# THE
# LEADERSHIP
# LIFECYCLE

# THE
# LEADERSHIP
# LIFECYCLE

### HOW TO **PREPARE**, HOW TO **EXCEL**, AND WHEN (AND HOW) TO EFFECTIVELY **EXIT!**

## W. JAMES WEESE, PH.D.

ARCHWAY
PUBLISHING

This book is a work of non-fiction. Unless otherwise noted, the author and the publisher make no explicit guarantees as to the accuracy of the information contained in this book and in some cases, names of people and places have been altered to protect their privacy.

Archway Publishing books may be ordered through booksellers or by contacting:

Archway Publishing
1663 Liberty Drive
Bloomington, IN 47403
www.archwaypublishing.com
844-669-3957

ISBN: 978-1-6657-4553-6 (sc)
ISBN: 978-1-6657-4555-0 (hc)
ISBN: 978-1-6657-4554-3 (e)

Library of Congress Control Number: 2023911272

Print information available on the last page.

Archway Publishing rev. date: 01/25/2024

# CONTENTS

# ABOUT THE AUTHOR

Dr. Jim Weese is a prominent leadership expert, a gifted speaker, and a community leader. He teaches and conducts research at one of Canada's top universities, where he has also excelled in a number of senior leadership roles. He has also consulted with some of the most admired companies in the world.

Weese is a Professor of Leadership and the former Dean of the Faculty of Health Sciences (2004-2015) at The University of Western Ontario (now known as Western University) in London, Ontario, Canada. He has also served as the Special Advisor to the Provost and as the Acting Associate Vice-President (International) at Western on two occasions. He was the Dean of the Faculty of Human Kinetics (1999-2004) at the University of Windsor prior to moving to Western in 2004. He is a transformational leader who has garnered impressive results in a variety of senior leadership positions throughout his distinguished career. He has engaged and informed audiences across many sectors on the merits of a team approach to leadership. His *5C Concept of Leadership* serves as the foundation to his approach to leadership.

Weese teaches, consults, conducts research, and delivers speeches on the topic of leadership. He is recognized and heralded as a transformational academic leader and a leading authority in the area whose research papers appear in the top journals in his field. He is a dynamic speaker who has delivered a number of scholarly and keynote addresses to national and international audiences as well as to practitioners who find his content and delivery style to be highly relevant and scalable. He is the author of a number of publications, including the highly acclaimed ***The 5C Leader: Exceptional Leadership Practices for Extraordinary Times***. He has engaged and inspired academic and professional audiences across many sectors with the contents of that book. The book has been warmly embraced for its conceptual strength and its heightened level of applicability.

He has served as a leadership consultant with both non-profit organizations as well as multinational companies, including the Ford Motor Company and General Motors of Canada, and he delivers academic leadership workshops through Academic Impressions, Inc. He currently serves as the Founding Executive Director of the Western Leader Academy, an intensive leadership development program designed to develop current and future academic leaders.

He has served in a number of senior leadership positions during his career, including serving as the President of the North American Society for Sport Management and President of the National Deans Councils for both Kinesiology (CCUPEKA) and Health Sciences Deans (CAHSD). He has been an active volunteer and board member with a number of boards and agencies in his city, province and country.

He has earned a number of academic and leadership awards throughout his distinguished career including the top research and leadership awards from his profession, the Queen's Jubilee Medal from the Government of Canada in 2002 for his academic leadership and ten years later, the Queen's Diamond Jubilee Medal in recognition for his leadership and advocacy for exercise and physical activity. The North American Society for Sport Management awarded him a Research Fellowship (in the inaugural group), as well as the prestigious Dr. Earle F. Zeigler Award in 2001, the Dr. Garth Paton Distinguished Service Award in 2015, and the Distinguished Sport Management Educator Award in 2022. In 2010, Weese worked with the Men's and Women's Olympic Hockey Teams at the Winter Olympic Games in Vancouver, Canada, and he was recently appointed by the Government of Canada to serve as the Vice-Chair of the Legacy Fund Allocation Committee charged with the allocation of the surplus and investment funds left over from Canada hosting the Pan American Games. In 2014, his alma mater, the University of Windsor inducted him into its Sports Hall of Fame and eight years later, awarded him the prestigious Alumni Award of Merit.

Dr. Weese lives in London, Ontario, Canada with his wife, Sherri. His passions include golf, hockey, guitar, and gardening.

# DEDICATION

To Sherri, my wife, soulmate, and
incomparable "editor in residence."

To our exceptional kids, Zach and Haylee.

To my parents, Doreen and Bill – departed but always remembered.

To my many students, past and present, who continue
to inspire me with their intelligence and energize
me with their insights and enthusiasm.

To all … my profound thanks.

# ACKNOWLEDGEMENTS

I have benefited from the insights and research findings of many capable graduate students through the years. I have only had one study focus on the end stage of the leadership lifecycle. I am deeply indebted to Jonathan FemiCole, who completed a Major Research Paper with me on the topic of the leadership lifecycle. Jonathan uncovered some of the limited research literature on the inevitable end stage of the leadership lifecycle. I acknowledge him and thank him for his contributions to this project. I also want to acknowledge the work of another student, Kevin Gruber, who assisted me with understanding and uncovering some of the latest research findings related to leader development, leader succession planning, and onboarding incoming leaders as a way of easing their transition into the role allowing them to "hit the ground" running.

I also want to acknowledge my friend and colleague Andy Hrymak, who, as Provost, invited me to develop and lead the Western Leader Academy as its Founding Executive Director. I am deeply appreciative of his creating this opportunity. The assignment immersed me in the leader development literature, and much of that literature supports the contents and suggestions outlined in this book. I acknowledge his vision and foresight to develop the Western Leader Academy, and I thank him for the confidence he showed in me to develop and deliver the program. I am very optimistic about the future of Western University given the quality of current and emerging academic leaders who participated in the Western Leader Academy Program. The "bench is deep" with talent, energy, and enthusiasm. The speakers and participants brought together in this program have also taught me a great deal about leader development and effectiveness.

I have been the beneficiary of learning from many great leaders across a number of organizations and industries throughout my career. I watched them, studied their practices, and asked them penetrating questions about their experience. Their insights were exceptionally helpful as I pieced together my final thoughts for the contents of this book. In fact, many of their insights are explicitly profiled in the pages of this text. They demonstrated, through their words and their actions, how great leaders make a difference and make it look easy. These leaders opened doors of opportunity for me, mentored me, and showed me the way. I watched, with admiration, how they effectively led their units, and when the time was right, I also watched them arrive at the conclusion that it was time for them to move on and seamlessly climb another mountain. They paid attention to the signals, and when they knew that the time was right, they left the leadership role with grace and dignity and with their legacies intact. They left the unit, organization, or institution that they were leading in much better shape than it was when they entered the leadership role (a.k.a. the true test of leadership), and their organizations were primed and positioned for sustained success long after their departure. It is a privilege to have worked with them, and I am proud to share some of their practices, insights, and examples in the pages of this book.

As per my practice, when I am developing the concept of a new book, I "test drove" some preliminary thoughts on my leadership lifecycle model at speaking engagements with audiences of all ages and from a number of different industries. Many of these individuals commented that this concept was new ground for them, and these phases need to be covered. I was inspired and encouraged by their reactions, and I embarked on writing this book largely based on their enthusiasm and support.

I hope that this book helps aspiring leaders prepare, and subsequently emerge into leadership roles. I also hope that it helps them heighten their effectiveness when they are in this role. I hope that leaders wishing to stay on in the role are inspired to adopt the recommended practices that will extend their efficacy and effectiveness as a leader. I also hope that the contents of the book helps leaders identify and appropriately respond to the signs and signals that it might be time for a change. Do they need to make significant changes or might it be time for them to depart the role and pursue other interests and challenges? If they do decide to depart, I trust that leaders will adopt the advice outlined in this book so they can do so with both grace and dignity and in a manner that helps ensure that their unit/organization continues to thrive. I have watched great leaders emerge, excel, and, when the time was right, depart with their legacies intact and their units primed for sustained success and prosperity. Isn't that something all leaders should aspire to attain? The best ones get all three stages of the leadership lifecycle right.

I hope that this book gives current leaders and aspiring leaders the tools, insights, and direction needed to emerge, excel, and when the time is right, appropriately depart leadership roles. It is possible and desirable.

Lead on, colleagues!!!

# PREAMBLE

Response to *The 5C Leader: Exceptional Leadership Practices for Extraordinary Times* book has been remarkable. I couldn't be more pleased. The book was authored to make a difference, and it has clearly succeeded. I endeavored to synthesize the vast leadership resource base into a simplistic but conceptually strong concept that students, leadership scholars, and current/aspiring leaders could understand and immediately put into practice. The book has also played well with members of the media and consumers who like to digest content through e-books or podcasts. Based on the responses of readers and those offered by people attending a campus or community speaking engagement, the book has more than met the mark. Readers and audience members seem to like the practicality and utility of the 5C concept.

It has been a great pleasure responding to readers and audience members attending my speaking engagements. I was pleased when many took the time to tell me that the book has made a difference for them. However, I noticed that three questions seem to consistently emerge from these interactions, namely:

1. *What can I do to best prepare and position myself for future leadership opportunities?*
2. *What can I do to work these 5C concepts into my leadership practices?*
3. *What can I do to get my boss to read this book and apply the concepts? Some phrased it as, "Can you sign this book and make it out to my boss? He (or She) really needs to read it."*

I reflected deeply on these three questions, and they prompted me to delve into this book project. I was convinced that many people had similar questions. How can leaders best prepare and position themselves for leadership opportunities (i.e., addressing question #1)? How can leaders embed the 5C Leader concepts into their day-to-day leadership practices (i.e., addressing question #2)? Finally, it is clear that too many practising leaders don't accurately read the signals that their influence is waning, and they must either change their practices or depart from the role and move on to new challenges. What are the signs and signals that a leader's impact is diminishing, and how and when do they know that it might be time for them to change (or consequently, be changed)? Rather than let others make decisions about them, how can leaders get ahead of the process and either change or depart the leadership role and do so with grace, dignity, and the assurance that the organization will continue to move forward (i.e., addressing question #3). These areas needed further reflection and exploration and, in my view, warranted a book addressing the topics. I came up with the Lifecycle of Leadership model (presented in Figure 1). As noted, I developed and shared the concept with students, colleagues, and audiences at my speaking engagements. Feedback on the concept was universally positive. People connected with the concept, and I was further convinced that it filled a void in the literature and it was meeting an acute need in practice.

The concept clearly resonated with those who aspired to leadership roles. These people wanted clear guidance on what they could do to prepare themselves for opportunities that they envisioned for their future. Their focus was clearly on the early stages of the model. Practicing leaders seemed to enjoy reflecting on their preparation for leadership. Many shared that they reflected on their preparation, and many commented that they followed similar stages through strategic planning or in many cases, pure luck. However, they seemed to gravitate to the middle stages of the model. They wanted clear, cogent, and practical information that would help them be more effective in the leadership role. While social media feeds, TED Talks, blogs, and bookstore shelves are filled with content designed to help leaders heighten their effectiveness, some admitted that the information could be overwhelming and complex. I shared my simple, but conceptually strong leadership practices with practicing leaders, and they enthusiastically embraced them. Many shared that they wanted to put them in play as soon as possible. I have always believed that the leadership literature could be distilled and simplified into a model that was practical and scalable and, hopefully, facilitating readers soaring in the leadership role. It remains my hope that these practices will help leaders maximize their impact over a longer period of time. However, in reality, the end comes for all leaders, and it was crystal clear to me that very little content exists to help leaders effectively navigate the later stages of the leadership lifecycle. Yes, All leaders eventually depart the leadership role. Some are pushed. Some are pulled. Fewer leave on their terms, with their units flourishing and positioned for sustained success (and their stakeholders wanting more). My goal is to help leaders and their units or organizations realize this positive endpoint.

There is a leadership lifecycle, and my goal was to help current and aspiring leaders effectively navigate each stage of their leadership journey. Many participants in my leadership seminars stated that the leadership lifecycle model resonated with them. I could see it in their eyes and in their body language. Many participants publicly or privately admitted that they could have used some guidance to help them effectively navigate through the earlier and midpoint stages of the leadership lifecycle model. I was especially moved by the reaction of those nearing the end of their tenures. These leaders desperately sought advice on effectively navigating this stage in their lifecycle. This revelation proved to be a nirvana moment for me. This was all the motivation I needed to delve into the research literature, sprinkle in my experience and the experience of colleagues that I interviewed, and craft a new book, entitled *The Leadership Lifecycle: How to Prepare; How to Excel, and When (and How) to Effectively Exit.*

Musicians and authors alike counsel writers to focus on the things that they know. Relationships and family are the usual themes of songs from Ed Sheeran and Taylor Swift. John Grisham has transitioned from a courtroom lawyer to a best-selling author of novels focused on courtroom dramas. Former crime reporter Patricia Cornwall pivoted from a career as an investigative journalist to a best-selling author of crime novels. Jazz trumpeter Dizzy Gillespie may have said it best when he eloquently and accurately proclaimed that *"if you haven't lived it, it won't come out of the horn."* I have certainly lived the leadership lifecycle.

Figure 1.

The Lifecycle of Leadership

1. Preparation Phase
2. Launch Phase
3. Maturity Phase
4. Rebirth/Renewal or Time to Exit
5. Graceful and Effective Exit and Transition to the Next Challenge

As a young academic, I set myself on a path to secure leadership positions in higher education. I felt that I had the skills and motivation to lead. I knew that I needed to prepare myself for roles long before they became available. I benefitted from incredible role models, mentors, and sponsors who showed me the way, coached me, and opened doors of opportunity for me so I could get the right experiences. My knowledge, confidence, and experience profile all grew. Once in the mid-level and senior academic leadership roles, I adopted and implemented the six practices outlined in the middle section of the model in this book. Finally, and on two occasions, I departed senior academic leadership roles for other opportunities when I felt that the time was right for me to move on. However, I also wrestled with the decisions and the inevitable uncertainty that many encounter when deciding to leave a role that they enjoy so much. That said, I knew in my heart that it was time to move on. I had done all that I could do in these roles, and I was sure that the units I was leading were on a solid platform for the next leader to assume the reins.

I helped prepare potential successors through a series of leader development experiences even though I knew that I would have no influence on the final selection of my successors. Once named, I helped onboard my successors and then strategically did my best to stay out of their way once they assumed the leadership role. At the time of my departure, I also ensured that I had something else to look forward to and strategically embarked on the processes outlined in the final stage of the leadership lifecycle model. I lived it, and based on the clairvoyant observations of Dizzy Gillespie, I was able to "let it flow from my horn." However, experience alone doesn't qualify someone to write a book that will hopefully make a difference for others. This book is also based on my research and informed by the latest research of others who have studied leadership emergence, leadership effectiveness, and leadership succession planning. The book is designed to help facilitate success at all stages of the leadership life cycle, and help leaders effectively and strategically navigate each stage in the journey.

Those aspiring to leadership roles will be able to reflect on their preparation and adopt empirically validated strategies to best prepare for leadership roles and position themselves for opportunities. Those currently in leadership roles can use the tried-and-true leadership practices and make necessary adjustments to heighten their success in the role. Last but not least, leaders can assess their impact by more effectively identifying the unobtrusive signals that their leadership impact is waning. They can commit to making the necessary adjustments to reinvigorate their effectiveness or make the decision to effectively depart from the role and move on to new challenges and invigorating opportunities. Regardless of the decision made, these leaders can help ensure that they manage the decision while ensuring that a strong and effective leadership development program is in place to facilitate a smooth and successful succession. Leaders want to leave their units in better shape than it was upon their entry, leave the role with pride and dignity, and ensure that the unit they are leading is positioned to springboard into future success.

> Leave everyone you meet better than you found them. Become an encourager of potential versus a destroyer of confidence.
>
> —ROBIN SHARMA

I wish readers well in this incredible and exciting journey. Onward!!!

W. James Weese
2023

# THE PREPARATION PHASE

## A READER'S GUIDE:

Upon reading this section, readers will understand:

- that leadership can be learned;
- the experience and preparation needed to effectively emerge and excel in leadership roles;
- the undeniable role that role models, mentors, and sponsors can play in leader development;
- the importance of emotional intelligence to leadership and what areas need to be developed;
- the importance of early stretch assignments and disciplined reflection to leader development;
- the importance of building a broad and balanced experience profile to heighten leader development;
- the importance of remaining a "work in progress", and;
- the need to find your voice and trust your abilities.

Why do some people emerge into leadership roles, and others seem to never get there? Are some people natural-born leaders? Can leaders be developed, and if so, how? This portion of the book summarizes the leader development literature and provides an answer to the burning question that I frequently get at my leadership seminars and presentations, namely, "how can I become a leader?" In the pages below, I outline the key steps people need to follow to prepare themselves for leadership opportunities when they become available (and as noted in the next Chapter, I will offer suggestions for sustained success in the role once they arrive). Readers will be introduced to the research literature surrounding the age-old question of "are leaders born or made," and hopefully, readers will understand that while both elements are factors that contribute, having the opportunity and possessing a desire to assume the leadership role is also important. Leadership is hard work and not for the faint of heart. Leaders must be selfless, disciplined, and willing to make difficult decisions. Not everyone wants to make these commitments. However, those who do will be well served by the contents of this book as they effectively and strategically navigate their journey.

> Many want to be leader, but far fewer want to do leader. Leadership is much more than a prestigious title.

A recent Gallup Poll[1] suggested that great leaders inspire and motivate others; confidently address and overcome challenges; effectively forge relationships; are personally accountable and hold others to account, and; make good decisions that are organizationally focussed. However, the same poll indicated that less than 20 percent of employees possess these attributes. Clearly, more leaders need to be developed. Organizations need a deeper bench of potential leaders. But how? Are some born with these skills and talents? Are others developed to lead? Might there be a combination of factors and other elements at work? These questions, and others, will be explored in the following section.

Life isn't about finding yourself. Life is about creating yourself.

— GEORGE BERNARD SHAW

## ARE LEADERS BORN OR MADE?

The question of whether leaders are born or made is as old as the study of leadership. Some could effectively argue that the trait theory of leadership implies that those who emerge and are effective in leadership roles owe their privilege to their genetic makeup. After all, researchers[2] have confirmed that leaders are often generally taller, more confident, usually more extroverted, and emotionally intelligent.

The late Dr. Warren Bennis[3] weighed in on the born-made debate by emphatically stating that, of course, leaders are born, as are zookeepers, garbage collectors, and astronauts. Bennis believed that what an individual did with their talents was far more important than their genetic composition. I agree. Another leadership legend, the late Dr. Bernard Bass[4], concurred by noting that genetic gifts like intelligence, emotional stability, energy, and some physical gifts might give an individual the genetic predisposition to lead but by no means determines who emerges or who doesn't emerge. History books and the popular press are inundated with examples of leaders who might fit this profile but do not emerge or succeed as a leader, and others who do not fit the profile but do subsequently emerge or succeed as a leader. These conflicting findings ultimately led to the demise of the trait theory of leadership, but perhaps the theory was prematurely discarded.

> Today, effective leadership is commonly viewed as central to organizational success, and more importance is placed on leadership development than ever before.[5]

Scholars have tackled this born vs. made question in many ways, but perhaps the most compelling evidence emerges from research conducted with identical twins (i.e., studying the lives and leadership paths of identical twins raised separately). This natural experiment has allowed researchers to specifically distinguish the role of genetics and the role of opportunity and development. One such study[6] of 12,112 twins from Sweden suggested that genetics played a significant role in leadership emergence (44% of the variance for women and 37% of the variance for men). Other twin study researchers have calculated the genetic influence at 30% for males[7] and 32% for females.[8]

> Good raw materials are critical to success.
>
> —PLATO

There appears to be some agreement among researchers that genetics and experience <u>both</u> play a role in the development and emergence of leaders. Some attach a percentage breakdown of the role that nature and nurture play in explaining who emerges and succeeds in leadership. A 2012 study published by the Centre for Creative Leadership[9] concluded that senior leaders believe that (leaders are 19.1% born, 54.2% made and 28.5% equally born <u>and</u> made). Other theorists have produced similar percentages (i.e., 24% born; 76% made). Some scholars[10] have combined the factors and concluded that the genetic influences are less pronounced for leaders raised in families with higher family socioeconomic status and those with stronger parental support than leaders raised in poorer conditions or in less supportive environments. In these cases, the impact of genetics was found to be more pronounced.

> You are destined to become the person you decide to be.
>
> —RALPH EMERSON WALDO

Based on the research evidence, I believe that leaders are both born <u>and</u> made. Each plays a part in explaining who emerges and succeeds and who doesn't. Good raw materials are essential, as is a conceptually strong leader development program with a high premium on understanding values, character, technology, emotional intelligence, globalization, reflection, and organizational culture. Leaders can also be effectively developed through their exposure to strong role models, mentors, and sponsors. However, I would also add that luck, opportunity, and a desire to lead also play an underappreciated role in the emergence process.

> Your actions, not your words, define character.
>
> —ARISTOTLE

## IMPORTANCE OF OPPORTUNITY

Being born into a family that provides strong role models, balances challenge with support, ensures exposure to enriching educational and enrichment opportunities, and access to a strong social network can't be overlooked as a significant contributor to leader development. Children with parents, siblings, peers, and influencers who challenged and encouraged them enjoyed incredible leader development benefits. These individuals were simply born into the right family and at the right time. Some scholars [11] have refined the role that genetics and experiences play in a leader's development by looking at the interaction of these variables given family circumstances. They have concluded that the genetic influence on leader development is less when children are raised in supportive family environments where enrichment opportunities are plentiful. Conversely, the genetic impact was found to be more pronounced for leaders born into less stable, less affluent family environments.

Factors as simple as birth order (i.e., firstborns) have been linked with higher achievement, higher levels of dominance, and leadership emergence, skills often honed and tempered by teaching and guiding their younger siblings[12]. Firstborns usually serve as role models, mentors, and protectors of their younger siblings.[13] That said, who can orchestrate their birth order? Luck and opportunity are inextricably linked.

Contemporary leadership theory that calls for a more collaborative approach to leadership (e.g., leadership teams, participative and servant leadership) might benefit later-born siblings. Research[14] suggests that later-born children are generally more relationship-oriented than their first-born siblings. Again, who has the power to dictate their birth order? Luck plays a significant part in the process. There are other factors that contribute to leadership emergence. Being at the right place at the right time is also a factor that is often overlooked as a factor in explaining how one person emerges and/or excels in a leadership role. Those with great potential to lead may not get the opportunity if there is a long line of candidates also interested in limited leadership roles. Conversely, those born into situations where fewer candidates exist for leadership roles will find greater opportunities for leadership emergence. David Foot[15] eloquently and effectively highlights this reality in his insightful *Boom, Bust and Echo* book. Leadership opportunities and competition for these roles may be more readily available for some due to the timing and location of their births. As a result, luck may be an underappreciated factor for emerging leaders.

In the final analysis, genetic composition, development, and luck all appear to be factors that influence leader development and emergence. I would add that a desire to lead is another factor that is underappreciated in the leadership development research base. Many people have the genetic gifts and the experience required to lead, but lack the passion and desire to lead. Leadership is not for the faint of heart. Some choose not to lead. They don't want the responsibility or the headaches that often come with leadership. If this is the case, it is the right choice for them given the demands leaders face. Effective leaders must be "all-in." Let's further explore the role that a desire to lead plays in leader development and emergence.

# HAVING THE DESIRE TO LEAD

Candidates for leadership must also have the desire to serve in the leadership role. Some have all the attributes, opportunities, and experiences but lack the desire to assume the responsibilities (and headaches) that go with the leadership role. Motivation, energy, and a willingness to serve others are prerequisites to leadership and factors that are not often mentioned in the nature/nurture debate. These leaders have a strong desire to achieve, not for their own gain, but for the success of the group. However, in my opinion, a desire to lead and a willingness to assume leadership opportunities and commensurate levels of stress and demands that come with leadership are often overlooked factors. Effective leaders are driven to succeed. They have unbridled enthusiasm and a commitment to improvement. Setbacks are not viewed as failures but, more accurately, as opportunities to improve. These leaders shine a light on failures as a way of turning them into learning opportunities. They keep score. They measure performance against predetermined targets. They share success for achievement and are not afraid to shoulder the blame when appropriate. Finally, they display heightened levels of enthusiasm and a strong motivation to lead.

> Failing at something means that you are challenging yourself. Reflect on the experience, use it as a learning experience, and be better the next time opportunity emerges.

# PREPARING TO LEAD

Given the importance of development, let's now turn our attention to some of the factors that play a role in preparing young people to lead. Researchers have studied the early years, the adolescent years, and the higher education years and identified key opportunities and experiences available to aspiring leaders at the right time, and concluded that they are fundamental to leader development. Let's take a look at these critical years.

> Tell me, what is it you plan to do with your one wild
> and precious life?
>
> —MARY OLIVER

## THE EARLY YEARS

Robert Fulghum[16] had it right in his magnificent and clairvoyant book *All I Really Needed to Know I Learned in Kindergarten: Uncommon Thoughts on Common Things.* Contemporary leadership theorists state that leaders must engage others, treat people well, be honest, reflect on their actions and be curious. Fulghum suggested that we learned these things as five-year-old Kindergarten students. I agree. Opportunities to play constructively with others, to work out differences, and to treat others with respect and dignity are key parts of Kindergarten and leadership success throughout the lifespan. Children can learn valuable lessons on the playground, in schoolyards, and in activities undertaken with other children. Leader development expert David Day suggested that cognitive development and the social skills (what we call emotional intelligence) required for leader emergence and success are often developed through play and social contact in these developmental years.[17] Children placed in these situations can learn to engage others, work cooperatively with them toward shared outcomes, and develop the courage and confidence needed for leadership. These opportunities are so important to their development. Parents, siblings, coaches, teachers, and community leaders can make such a difference in the lives of children by creating rich learning opportunities for play and engagement and helping children learn leadership strategies that will serve them well in the future. These skills, developed and refined in children, can be invaluable to leader emergence and leader success in later years.[18] These programs play a much larger role than just keeping kids occupied. They are fundamental to their development and personal growth.

Growing up in the small, Canadian town of Dresden, Ontario (population 2,400) provided me with unlimited opportunities for leader development – in the playgrounds, at school, in sports environments, and in community programs. Play was uninhibited. My parents just told me to be home before dark. The parents of my friends also looked out for me, and my parents reciprocated for them. My coaches and program leaders were always encouraging and supportive, which encouraged me to learn, take calculated risks, and have the confidence to persevere in challenging times. I learned to cooperate and be a team player with my friends. Playground disputes were minimized, and when they sprung up, they were quickly and effectively resolved. We learned strategies for dealing with others for mutual benefit.

> The biggest risk is not taking any risk. In a world that's changing really quickly, the only strategy that is guaranteed to fail is not taking risks.
> —MARK ZUCKERBERG

I worry that some of these experiences are not as plentiful to today's generation of children. While there may be more opportunities vis-à-vis formal programs than in my day, these programs are usually governed, and often managed, if not over-managed, by adults. There is also significant formality to these programs. Don't get me wrong. We need parents and adult support and leadership, and I know that they are well-intentioned and want what is best for their children and those in the group. However, at times, they can get too involved. Research supports this claim. For example, researchers have determined that children of parents who support them but don't get too involved in solving their problems demonstrate greater leadership practices as adults.[19] Furthermore, overly engaged parents, often described as "helicopter parents," can stunt leader development in their children, depress their self-esteem, and lower their confidence levels.[20]

There is only one way to avoid criticism: Do nothing, say nothing, and be nothing.

—ARISTOTLE

As a parent and a youth sport coach, I always felt that it was important to build resilience in kids. Children need the space, guidance, and opportunity to resolve differences personally. Parents can teach their children how to effectively reflect on a situation and determine if they handled the situation correctly. They could also reflect on what they might do differently the next time if presented with the same set of circumstances. Parents can also help children rehearse situations in advance, so they have the skills, strategies and confidence needed to effectively manage them. These skills practices can help children be more effective in resolving differences in addition to developing their leadership skills for the present and future.

As a practicing leader, I often needed to take time to reflect on situations and try to understand the motives behind the actions of others. I often rehearse how I will handle the situation and I try to anticipate how the conversations will go. I have found this strategy to be an effective tool in engaging in difficult but critical conversations. After engaging in these challenging conversations or after making a tough decision, I routinely take the time to reflect on the outcome and decide if my course of action was effective. If not, I think about what I would do the next time when confronted with a similar situation. As noted throughout this book, rehearsal and reflection are powerful leadership tools, and teaching children and adolescents how to effectively rehearse and reflect, and then take responsibility for the consequences, are gifts that will help them in the moment, and later, in both life, and in leadership. I believe that these approaches have served me, and those in my circle well – and they will for you are yours as well.

If it doesn't challenge you, it won't change you.

—TIM KIGHT

## THE ADOLESCENT YEARS

The adolescent years are a time of rapid growth (i.e., physically, emotionally, and cognitively). It can be a challenging time for young people as they form an identity and their place in the world. Social comparisons are omnipresent and accelerated in society today through ever-present social media channels. It can often be a challenging time, especially for females. That is why engagement in group activities, led by leaders who ensure inclusivity and engagement are so important to leader development. It can be a time when true leaders can emerge and refine their leadership skills and ensure that others are engaged and feel supported. As their skill levels develop and their interests become more refined, adolescents have the opportunity to participate in a variety of group activities like sports, student government, community groups, clubs, etc. This involvement should be encouraged, for enrichment purposes, but also for leader development benefits.[21] Researchers have the impact of these types of activities on leader development and the results are quite promising. For example, researchers have studied this question and uncovered positive results that should comfort program leaders. In addition, researchers have found a strong, positive predictive relationship between participation in team sports and community groups (e.g., boy scouts and girl guides) and leader emergence in the future.[22] Critics were justifiably current in highlighting the limitations of these descriptive studies and the need to engage in experimental research studies to determine the precise impact of these programs on leader development. They would be correct in suggesting that perhaps stronger leaders are drawn to these programs in the first place, therefore negating the positive impact of the experience on leader development. I agree that a more refined experimental research paradigm is warranted, but these research findings, and others offer promise and do not detract from my strong advocacy for our role in building citizens and helping young people develop and refine their leadership skills.

## THE HIGHER EDUCATION YEARS

As young people enter their college and university years, even more opportunities for leader development are put in front of them. In addition to maturing intellectually and socially, young people at this age have opportunities to take credit and non-credit courses in leadership to understand the theoretical developments behind the concept. My students also receive diagnostic assessments (e.g., 5C Leadership Assessments[23]) of their leadership practices so they know their leadership strengths and areas in need of development. College and university courses in leadership have proven helpful in developing leaders of the future.[24] The post-secondary school experience also provides a plethora of opportunities for leader development and refinement. The college and university years are times for self-development and personal exploration. Students are generally on their own for the first time in their lives. They have to make their own decisions and are responsible for the outcomes of their choices. Greater levels of independence require heightened levels of discipline. Students are also exposed to a wide variety of formal and informal opportunities to help them develop and/or refine their leadership skills and potential. Western University (my employer) boasts 40 varsity teams, 19 Recreation clubs, and over 180 special interest clubs for students (https://www.uwo.ca/campus_life/clubs_associations.html) to engage in this type of development. Some of the larger universities across North America offer even larger co-curricular programs for enrichment and development.

# A COMMITMENT TO LIFELONG LEARNING

> "Leaders who keep learning may be the ultimate source of sustainable competitive advantage."[25]

Throughout my academic career as a professor and academic leader, I have followed students and alumni and watched their development with pride and interest. I have followed up more observational processes with penetrating questions (especially to graduates experiencing leadership success in their careers). I have watched students develop and refine their leadership skills in a variety of co-curricular pursuits like inter-university athletics[26], student government[27], clubs, community-engaged learning programs, and campus recreation, to name but a few. I have also researched leader development in students and student-athletes. [28] Later, as a Dean, I would visit with these students, now graduates, who would routinely point to their involvement in these types of programs, and without prompting, talk about how the experiences helped prepare them for success in leadership in work and life. While these graduates impressed me with their successes in their lives and careers, it also dawned on me that these graduates never stopped learning. They all seemed to be engaged in professional development activities that kept them current and aware of trends in their field and in the area of leadership. They remained curious and hungry for new learning opportunities. I believe that this is critical to success in leadership, and this observation helped form the last section of this book. Leaders must remain a "work in progress" and always be eager for new content and continual growth and development.

My academic colleagues and I can list a multitude of top students we have taught through the years who excelled academically and appeared destined for career success. However, in spite of this early promise, a number of them subsequently struggled in their careers. We can also list an abundant number of average students (with respect to academic performance) who have soared in their lives and careers. As a professor and, later, Dean, I visited with many graduates and have often reflected on the ingredients that seemed to be fueling and facilitating their success. I frequently concluded that these graduates had something different that separated them from their less successful, less fulfilled counterparts. It wasn't their academic performance as students that set them apart, although they were all bright and they all graduated. I initially thought that personality was the differentiating feature. I remembered these professionals as students and remembered how they seemed to connect effortlessly with other students, staff, and faculty members. I recalled how they actively listened to others and demonstrated genuine respect for the perspectives of others. I remembered them being immensely popular as students. These attributes seemed to be serving them well as their lives and careers unfolded in the subsequent years. They seemed happy, content, and excited about the future. Their careers were taking off. As I probed deeper, I uncovered the transformative work of Daniel Goleman and colleagues, who introduced me to the concept of emotional intelligence.[29] That was the secret sauce that differentiated these students. It set them apart from their peers. As a result, I have been a strong supporter of the emotional intelligence area ever since, I have done my best to integrate it into

## AUTHOR EXPERIENCE

I have been a strong advocate for cocurricular experiences throughout my career because I have watched students grow and develop from the experience and go on to exceptional leadership careers upon graduation. I have also realized the benefits of these programs as a former two-sport varsity athlete.

I entered the University of Windsor in 1976 as a student seeking direction and purpose. My grades were not good, and my confidence level was low. In the summer between my first and second year I committed myself to training and making the varsity hockey team. My plan came to fruition. I was a fringe player on the team in my first year but I persevered and ended up as one of the team leaders as my career unfolded over the five years. As my role on the team grew, so did my confidence. My grades also soared. My confidence in social circles was commensurately elevated. I later earned a spot in our University's graduate program, and later earned a PhD from The Ohio State University. Along the way I developed a skill in a sport that I continue to enjoy into my mid 60s. Furthermore, as I reflect back on my enriching career as a University professor and leader, I know that so much of what I have accomplished was the result of my experience as a varsity hockey player. I have watched others follow my experience with the same results.

> Sports did it for me – but it can be any number of co-curricular activities where group members strive to attain a common goal. The leadership learning, especially if accompanied by a formal leadership development and deep reflection can be extremely valuable. I especially learned the value of discipline and hard work.

my leadership courses at the undergraduate and graduate levels. I design learning activities with my students to help develop their levels of emotional intelligence. Upon reflection, I have concluded that it might be the most important thing that I teach them in the time we spend together.

> People do not decide their futures. They decide their habits, and their habits decide their futures.
>
> —F. M. ALEXANDER

## DEVELOPING EMOTIONAL INTELLIGENCE

Measured as one's EQ, emotional intelligence is critical to engaging others on an emotional level, and consequently, it is the key to effective leadership. That was the secret sauce for these students. They used emotional intelligence to lead their lives, relationships, and careers. Goleman's research points to an 85% correlation between emotional intelligence (EQ) and executive leadership success. He further states that EQ is greater than IQ when it comes to leadership effectiveness. The higher a person moves in an organizational chart, the more important emotional intelligence becomes for future success. Great leaders inspire the hearts and minds of others, and they do it by deploying emotional intelligence.

> Engage the hearts of people, and their hands, feet, and brain will soon follow.

Perhaps the most encouraging aspect of emotional intelligence is the fact that it can be developed and refined. Aspiring leaders need to be proactive in active listening and be self-aware to know when they are not totally engaged or focused on hearing the perspectives of others. We can become better listeners if we are aware that we need help in the area and are motivated to make the change. We can take courses and workshops on active listening. A trusted mentor can be advised of the issue and provide coaching to leaders to better prepare them for conversations and meetings. Following these interactions, the coach and leader can deconstruct the exchange and monitor the degree to which the leader was engaged in active listening. I once had a leadership coach tell me that his trick was to be sure that the other person was finished before he responded. He worked hard to clearly absorb the viewpoints of the other person in the conversation. He would ask the person to elaborate or clarify as needed. He would play back what he thought he heard to the person and ask the person if he was hearing things accurately. Furthermore, he made it a practice to conclude the conversation when the other person felt it was completed, not when he did. This practice allowed him to sharpen his focus, and the other person in the conversation would feel that they were genuinely being heard. I adopted it, and it worked.

## A LIFE-LONG LESSON FROM A SENIOR PROFESSOR

Early in my academic career I was working away in my office when a senior colleague dropped by for a visit. He sat down in a chair beside my desk. We were having an engaging conversation when my office phone suddenly rang. I asked my colleague to hold for a minute while I took the call. I wrapped the call up as quickly as I could and returned my attention to my visitor.

He quickly, and sternly pointed out that I had picked up the ringing phone. I reminded him that it was ringing, but it had no impact on him. He reminded me that we were talking at the time and that it was impolite for me to have taken the call while we were engaged in our conversation. I had been conditioned to always answer an answering phone. However, he was right, and after apologizing for my action, I told him so. What a lesson! For the past 40 years, I don't answer a ringing phone when I am meeting with another person (unless I believe the call is an emergency - and emergency callers will immediately call back). I have passed on this lesson to younger colleagues and I hope that they will pass it on to those who they encounter.

Thanks Jack.

According to Goleman,[30] emotionally intelligent people have advanced levels of (1) self-awareness; (2) self-management, and (3) empathy, and leadership scholars suggest that emotionally intelligent leaders use these three elements to heighten their impact and efficacy. What is particularly heartwarming and encouraging for me is the fact that all three elements can be developed.[31]

The three critical areas of emotional intelligence are outlined below.

## DEVELOPING SELF-AWARENESS

According to Goleman and other EQ scholars[32], emotionally intelligent leaders have a high degree of self-awareness. They know their values and surround themselves with leaders who share their values. Strategy and activities are always open for debate, but not values. Emotionally intelligent leaders know what they stand for and against. Knowing your values and aligning them with your work can heighten motivation and bring meaning to the experience.

These types of leaders also read cues effectively and understand how they are perceived by others. They know their strengths and their areas of challenge. They are confident in their abilities. They have the ability to read and interpret their own emotions and how their words and actions are affecting others.

These types of leaders are not blindsided by developments in their group or industry because they are on top of issues and in constant communication with their colleagues. They have a strong sense of what they (and their group) can and cannot accomplish. They know their limits. They embrace constructive criticism. These leaders also have the ability to calibrate their impact on people and the unit that they are leading. They actively schedule a time to reflect on their activities and outcomes. They know that reflection is important to leadership as it gives them the opportunity to assess their impact, assess the impact of their direct reports, and take corrective action as needed.

Many of the respected leadership diagnostic instruments use self-other measurements (including the 5C Leadership Scale[33]) to determine a leader's strengths and areas of challenge. These instruments call for leaders to assess themselves, and superiors, peers, and direct reports are usually asked to provide their assessments of the leader's strengths and weaknesses (i.e., by completing the "other" version of the instrument. Researchers[34] have demonstrated that "other" measures are typically the most valid assessments (as opposed to self-assessments) as the "other" measures more favourably correlate to the most popular outcome measures of leadership research (i.e., member satisfaction and organizational effectiveness). A secondary analysis can be used to measure a leader's self-awareness by determining if statistically significant differences exist between the leader's assessment of their leadership strengths and weaknesses relative to the assessment of others (e.g., superiors, peers, and direct reports). Are their measures congruent or incongruent? Researchers[35] have proven that congruence between the self-other measures is critical to leadership effectiveness. However, this is a valuable method of assessing a leader's level of self-awareness. Self-awareness is the first part of Goleman's model of emotional intelligence and is an area that can be developed and refined. It is critical to success in the leadership role and consequently, should be a major part of leader recruitment and development. Reflection and coaching are underutilized strategies that can help prospective leaders develop their levels of self-awareness.

Seek to understand, not to be understood.
— STEPHEN COVEY

Self-aware leaders know that we all make mistakes, and upon re-flection, they will review situations and decisions made, reflect deeply on the outcome, and then determine what they might do differently in the future if presented with the same situation. When I am meeting candidates for leadership roles on my team, I always search for ways to gauge their level of self-awareness. I routinely ask candidates applying for leadership roles to share an experience where they made a mistake that led to a negative outcome. I often follow that up with a question about what they would do differently if they could be given a "mulli-gan". If candidates can't think of any mistakes that they have made, I immediately question their level of self-awareness. We have all made

## A LIFE-LONG LESSON FROM ANOTHER RESPECTED MENTOR

My first job out of university was as a recreation therapist at a treatment centre. The CEO was exceptional. She built great teams, ensured that we had a clear focus, ensured that we had the right skills to advance current and emerging priorities, and most of all, she connected effec-tively with colleagues.

One afternoon we were walking through the front office when a call came through to her. The receptionist took the call for a colleague and before patching the call through she innocently asked if she could tell the colleague who was calling. After passing the call through, the CEO politely, but forcibly asked the receptionist to discontinue the practice of asking who was calling. She said that it creates the impression that only important people will be put through and that it shouldn't matter who was calling. The call was important to the caller, and to the or-ganization. This was another great leadership practice that I quickly adopted and have maintained for over 40 years.

Thanks Connie.

mistakes and hopefully have recovered from them with the wisdom to do something else if presented with the same information a second time. Admitting that we made a mistake is not a sign of weakness, but it is an incredible sign of strength, self-awareness, and confidence. Being able to respond quickly to an alternative course of action speaks to their reflection activities. I want my candidates to quickly and confidently answer both questions. I look for it in those I want on the leadership teams surrounding me.

I continually ask my students to reflect on situations and collect as much information as they can to diagnose the dynamics of human interaction. We watch and deconstruct videos, analyze case studies, and I work with students to get them to open up about their feelings and how they believe that they are being perceived. One popular activity that I have used with my students to heighten their self-awareness and ensure that they do not rush to judgement is outlined below.

## AN ACTIVITY

### The Scene:

Your grandmother and you are flying from O'Hare Airport in Chicago to the Los Angeles International Airport in California. It will be a long flight, and to make the flight more enjoyable she asks you to take her to the airport early so she can purchase some cookies from a special Kiosk that has the exclusive rights to make and distribute these cookies. As her grandson you always want to please your Grandmother and as a result, you are sure that you get to the airport on time to make her special purchase. On the route there she talks more about the cookies than she does about the flight or the relatives who she is going to visit.

You arrive at the airport and while your grandmother waits in the Kiosk line for her cookies you head to the men's room. When you come out of the washroom you see that she is waiting for you and she can't wait to board the flight and delve into her three cookies.

### Concept check:

Students are asked if they understand the situation. They are asked if they have ever had a similar task of travelling with a grandparent? They are asked to speculate how the grandmother is feeling. They are asked how they are feeling as the travelling grandson.

### Act Two:

You both prefer aisle seats so you make your way to your seats. Luckily, you both have an empty seat between you. A middle aged man makes his way down the aisle and assumes the window seat beside your grandmother. The middle seat remains empty and will for the duration of the flight. The man is wearing a very expensive suit and appears to be on a business trip. Your grandmother stores her purse under the seat for takeoff and the plane is air born. You get out some schoolwork and begin to work on an essay that is due shortly after you get back home.

### Concept check:

Students are asked if they understand the situation and if they perceive anything out of the ordinary. We discuss the situation and ensure that students understand the context.

### Act Three:

About halfway through the flight you notice a cookie bag on the seat in-between your grandmother and the businessman. You know how much your grandmother enjoys the cookies and you can't wait to see her take her first bite. She opens the bag and takes one of the cookies. As you are watching her savour the cookie, you notice that the businessman is now reaching into the bag and he begins to eat one of the cookies. You cannot believe the nerve of this person. You are so angry, but you decide not to intervene. Both devour their cookie in record time. As your grandmother reaches for the third cookie, the businessman quickly puts his hand in the bag, takes the last cookie out, and breaks it in half, giving your grandmother one piece and taking the other. You watch in horror and disbelief.

### Concept Check:

Students are asked about how they feel having observed this situation and what they may have done had they been the grandchild in this situation. We discuss the options and I ask students to get in touch with their true feelings about the situation.

### Act Four:

Your grandmother is clearly agitated as are you. She doesn't say a word to the businessman throughout the remainder of the flight. When the plane lands, you both quickly grab your belongings and depart the plane. You consider bringing the situation to the attention of the flight attendant, but upon reflection decide to let it ride. As you enter the terminal you see a cookie kiosk and tell your grandmother that you will replace the cookies. You know that she is still angry so you offer to pay for the cookies. However, she insists on paying.

### Concept Check:

I check in with the students. Are they still feeling angry? What will they do if they encounter the businessman in the terminal? We discuss the options and alternatives.

### The Final Act:

The three cookies are placed in the bag and handed to your grandmother. She opens her purse to retrieve the funds, and much to her surprise, and yours, she sees the bag of cookies she purchased in Chicago. The treat she enjoyed on the plane actually belonged to the businessman who graciously shared his prized treat with your grandmother.

### Final Concept Check:

How do you feel now? What would you do now if you encountered the businessman in the terminal? We discuss the actions and the lessons learned on rushing to judgement and being more self-aware.

## DEVELOPING SELF-MANAGEMENT

Goleman[36] suggested that the second requisite skill of emotionally intelligent leaders is their ability to remain calm and focused, especially in times of stress and adversity. They don't act on impulses. They are, and are seen to be, honest, trustworthy, and values-driven. Being honest and trustworthy is the foundation of my 5C Leader model.[37] A house with a faulty foundation will soon crumble and fall to the ground. The same metaphor applies to leadership. Leaders who are dishonest, don't follow through on commitments, and can't be trusted, lack the foundation needed for long-term leadership success. These people might fool people initially, but like a house with a poor foundation, their influence and impact will soon come crashing down. My colleagues in the Ivey Business School at Western University reinforce this point with their insightful work on the topic of character and leadership.[38] . They highlight 11 character virtues (i.e., Courage, Drive, Collaboration, Integrity, Temperance, Accountability, Justice, Humility, Humanity, Transcendence, and Judgement), each of which can be quantitatively measured (self-assessment or assessments made by superiors, peers, or direct reports) using their valid and reliable Leadership Character Insight Assessment -360 (LCIA-360) questionnaire.[39]

> Character is more important than reputation because reputation may not be accurate.
>
> —JOHN WOODEN

Emotionally intelligent leaders are consistent and always honest and trustworthy. They manage themselves accordingly. While they also suffer setbacks and these disappointments can be discouraging, they are also mindful of the fact that colleagues look to them for leadership, optimism, and a positive path forward. These leaders understand that followers need them. They have the ability and insights to self-regulate their words and channel their activities in a positive fashion. They have the self-awareness to understand their emotional state, understand the triggers that bring negative emotions on, and have strategies (e.g., deep breathing, reflection, positive thinking) to manage these emotions before they derail their ability to influence. They appear to be in control and emotionally stable. Naturally, there are times when they are disappointed in people and results, but they are able to harness their emotions and present themselves in a positive and forward-seeking manner. Failures and disappointments are acknowledged and deconstructed so that they are not repeated in the future. Followers trust these leaders and value their positive mindset and optimistic approaches. These leaders embrace learning. Talented colleagues want to be part of groups and organizations with this type of trusted, supportive leader. These leaders manage themselves and their emotions accordingly and project a sense of calm that helps others confidently and effectively find a way forward. They role model consistent and reliable behaviour. They redirect disruptive behaviours and impulses in themselves and others. They engage colleagues in group problem-solving activities where appropriate. They can manage change because they are consistent and values-driven. In short, leaders with advanced levels of self-management control their emotions and feelings so they can guide others. They read cues (e.g., of others, of the situation) effectively and have the wisdom, confidence, and temperament to focus on the issue so they can manage the situation effectively. They don't allow their instincts to take over. They take a deep breath or two when needed, reflect on the situation and circumstances, and make thoughtful and deliberate comments and decisions. Conflicts are often "nipped in the bud" because these self-aware leaders are on top of situations and deal with them before they spin out of control.

Trust is earned, not given.

When conflict arises these leaders lean on the relationships that they have built with colleagues, and sometimes use humour, to disarm antagonists and channel energies into a more productive path forward. They show their vulnerability, and at times engage in self-deprecating behaviour to showcase their vulnerabilities. However, they remain in control of their emotions, and they don't let their impulses impact the moods and feelings of others. These leaders connect with people. They build strong relationships and can inspire colleagues to higher levels of achievement and group success. They can lead change when required, attract and retain high-quality members, and inspire those who come under their influence.

Excellence often happens on the other side of conflict.

## DEVELOPING EMPATHY

Empathy is best defined as the ability to understand and share the feelings of another person. Empathetic leaders have a high degree of intuition and are sensitive to the feelings and emotions of others. They can read the signals and thoughtfully consider impact of decisions and their words on the feelings and emotions of others. They are kind and considerate leaders who also get results. This approach to leadership is even more important given the advances in leadership and the quest to attract and retain the best talent. The best performers seek, if not demand, an emotionally intelligent leader who displays advanced levels of empathy. These performers will display unseen levels of loyalty and commitment to these types of leaders. They will be inspired to learn and develop under the influence of an emotionally intelligent leader who genuinely cares about them. Followers typically have a higher rapport with this type of leader and by extension, the organization as a result.

## A YOUNG DEAN'S INVESTMENT

University professors are bright, committed, and often opinionated. They can have strong feelings on issues. As a young Dean I realized that the best way forward for our Faculty was to have a stronger knit unit. While I wanted professors to debate issues because healthy conflict can lead to better decision making, I knew that there was a better way forward. I wanted professors to gather more informally. I wanted them to have coffee and lunch together, and to get to know each other on a deeper level. My hope was that they would gain a better understanding of each other's perspectives on issues. Even though times were economically challenging, we invested in a lounge that would bring people together socially.

It worked. I found that relationships and engagement improved. Tensions de-escalated. Colleagues got to know each other better and better understood the perspectives of others before gathering around a formal meeting table and dealing with issues. Our meetings became more focussed. We made better decisions and did so in a less aggressive and contentious manner. In hindsight, I was using my self-management skills to make a rational decision that resulted in positive change.

These leaders get to know their followers. They know about their colleagues' interests outside of the workplace. In many cases, they get to know their families. They ask questions because they care. They pay attention to what people are saying. They are genuinely friendly, supportive and caring. These attributes, and the manner with which they are displayed helps build strong bonds with colleagues and the relationship facilitates higher levels of mutual trust and commitment. These leaders engage and ignite others.

Your eyes leak so your head won't swell.
—VINCE GILL'S GRANDMOTHER'S REACTION
TO HIM BEING OVERTLY EMOTIONAL

Many organizations, including my own university are paying greater attention to stakeholder engagement. We know that we need leaders who can inspire greater performance by being more emotionally intelligent leaders. This type of leadership can cascade throughout a unit and institution and needs to if the organization is to maximize its potential. Leaders at Western University have worked with an industrial psychologist who periodically measures colleague engagement and provides detailed quantitative and qualitative assessments of areas of strength as well as those in need of attention. Informative graphs, colour-coded to draw attention to areas that have high, moderate, and low levels iof engagement are created. The consultant tabulates the results, meets with each academic leader and their team to deconstruct the results and helps the leader and leadership team develop a program of activities designed to heighten member engagement across all areas.

## IMPORTANCE OF REFLECTION SKILLS

Reflection is a powerful and underutilized process that helps facilitate personal growth and leader development. I met Mr. John Thomson when he served as the 20th Chancellor at my institution, Western University. I looked forward to the social events and dinners when I had the chance to sit with people like John and learn from their vast experience. John had served as the Chairman of the Board of TD Bank and as the Vice Chairman of the Board of the IBM Corporation. He also had experience as the President and Chief Executive Officer of IBM Canada. Suffice it to say that he had a wealth of experience to draw upon. At one of the dinners, John shared a practice with me that he had picked up from other successful leaders. Each week he would set aside one hour for uninterrupted reflection. His staff knew that this was protected time. During that hour, he would reflect on the progress that he was making as a leader and identify areas for change. He also reflected on the performance and developmental needs of his direct reports as well as the performance of the organization. I remember him saying: *"Jim, I have yet to meet a successful leader who didn't engage in a practice like this."* His words were clairvoyant. I knew that I needed to adopt this practice and counsel those whom I influence to do the same.

As a Dean, I immediately adopted this practice and shared it with other academic leaders in my workshops and seminars who have reported positive results from their implementation of the practice. For me, Friday afternoons worked the best, and I did this every second Friday. I may ask colleagues to provide me with data to review in advance of my session (e.g., student application data, incoming averages, publication records, research grant applications and success stories, research income, member engagement ratings, student satisfaction measures). I would reflect on my leadership practices and decisions and consider my development needs. I reflected on the performance of my direct reports and on their development needs. In summary, I took stock of what everything was adding up to. Were we making progress? What did we need to stop doing? What needed more attention? In my view, this practice is critical for leaders at every level. Without it, each day, each week, and each year bleeds into the next and before you know it, too much time is behind you.

I found the practice so helpful that I have brought it to other leadership roles I have assumed and to my personal life. I periodically set time aside to think about how I can be healthier and how things are going in my role as a husband, as a father, and with my friends. Do any of these areas need greater attention? I also reflect on my professional career and my community leadership and adjust as needed. Near the end of each calendar year, I also give myself a personal performance review, and I also map out my goals and strategies for the coming year. This reflective activity is critically important to me from both a personal and professional perspective, and I routinely recommend it to students, colleagues, and participants in my leadership seminars. Reflection is a big part of emotional intelligence, which, we now know is a critical component of leadership emergence and success. It can, and in my view, must be applied to our personal and professional lives.

The ability to reflect is especially important in leadership and, consequently must be built into a leader development program. Current and aspiring leaders need to understand the importance of reflection to effective leadership and be taught the mechanics of the process.

> "Critical to the success of any leadership development process is the ability to encourage participants to reflect on learning experiences in order to promote the transfer of knowledge and skills to work contexts."[40]

The research is also clear that leadership development is important and must be ongoing. Leaders can be developed and must be continually developed. Leaders must remain a work in progress. I have been involved in leader development programs for many years. I have led workshops and seminars in academic, corporate, and social service agencies. There are key practices that leaders must employ to heighten their success. They are effectively summarized in the next section of this book. However, before we get there, let's look at the leader development literature and the compelling evidence about how leaders can be made.

## A PLAN FOR LEADER DEVELOPMENT

The research is clear that leaders can also be developed through a series of strategic leader development programs.[41] Researchers like David Day[42] and his colleagues have been especially instrumental in assessing the impact of leader and leadership development programs. Day and his colleagues are especially effective in highlighting the key distinction between leader development (i.e., the personal skills, practices of individual leaders) and leadership development (i.e., an intact leadership team engaging in a program of development that has the potential to make the leadership team more effective). These two areas are differentiated as leader development/

leadership development. Leadership consultants and coaches need to make the distinction between the two concepts as they are often erroneously used interchangeably. Leader development can be facilitated by exposing individuals to a series of developmental experiences that make them more effective. They are often determined based on 360-degree feedback data (e.g., the 5C Leader Assessment Questionnaire is an example of a "self-other" instrument). Leaders complete the "self-version" of the instrument, and superiors, peers, and direct leaders complete the "other-version" of the instrument relative to the leader. Consultants and leadership coaches should immediately look for congruence between the measures, as well as high and low scores when developing a personalized plan of leadership development. Congruence is a measure of a leader's self-awareness. How do superiors, peers and subordinates perceive them and are their perceptions congruent with those of the leader? Ideally, the measures should be similar. If differences exist, it might point to a need for the leader to rethink their leadership practices as well as their level of self-awareness, which is a major component of emotional intelligence and as outlined earlier in the book, a critical component of emotional intelligence.

Another important analysis is to look at the strengths and weaknesses identified by the leader and those assessing the leader. Is there congruence between the measures? If not, why not. What areas are uniformly strong and need to be maintained? What areas are seen as weak and in need of development? Do different groups (e.g., subordinates vs. peers) rate the leader differently. If so, why might these differences exist? Areas of strength should be highlighted so leaders can continue engaging in these types of leader behaviors. Areas that are scored low warrant attention and conceptually designed programs to shore up those areas in need of development.

Current and future leaders need to understand the current trends in leadership and ensure that they are being prepared to meet current and emerging issues.[43] Advances in telecommunications is making the world a smaller, more connected place so future leaders must be globally aware of opportunities and threats. Current and future leaders will need to understand this interconnectivity and lead accordingly. Multiculturalism will increase due to rising immigration rates and global business strategies. Leaders will need to understand the implications and lead accordingly. Will they be prepared to do so? Technology will continue to advance and future leaders will undoubtedly be confronted with issues springing from automation and artificial intelligence. How will their leadership style adapt to these changes and the shifting landscape brought on by technology? Will they be adaptable as well as sufficiently prepared? Leaders of the future will need to be flexible and accommodating.

For example, look at the disruptive influence of the pandemic and how it has altered the rules of engagement for many organizations and leaders. More colleagues are now working from home and many of those who are not seek that opportunity. Some work in a hybrid model, and some are working permanently from home. How will leaders of the future engage colleagues who may not personally see as much (or at all)? How will they build an organizational culture when so many people are not physically present? Last but not least, how will they build, inspire, and engage great teams in a remote environment? Will they be prepared to lead in these environments? These are only a few of the areas and issues expected to confront leaders of today and tomorrow. They will need to be developed to stay current, anticipate trends, adapt, focus, engage and inspire colleagues with changing expectations and aspirations. It won't be easy. Strategic and on-going leader development will be essential.

Harvard professor and prolific author John Kotter has written extensively on leadership and leading change. His seminar article[44] on leader development has particular relevance and application for me and upon reflection, explains my journey as a leadership scholar and practitioner. He interviewed 200 successful leaders in a quest to determine the influences and experiences that helped shape them as leaders. Seven common themes emerged from his research (i.e., the value of tackling challenging assignments early in one's career; having inspiring role models; experiencing early task force assignments; having established leaders as mentors; being exposed to meetings and content outside of one's core responsibilities; engaging in leader development programs, and; learning experiences that are trial and error to know how to respond to situations). I have developed my own list of leader development activities based on my research and experience working with established leaders. I have shared these suggestions with my own children and a countless number of university students and alumni who seek leadership opportunities in their careers. I am happy to share them with you at this time. In my view, people aspiring to leadership roles need to:

## PURSUE AND EMBRACE GROWTH OPPORTUNITIES

> I never lose. Either I win, or I learn.
>
> —NELSON MANDELA

Take a moment and reflect on the assignments and experiences that you have assumed in your life. I have, and I have now concluded that the most challenging experiences also provided me with the best opportunity to grow, develop and springboard on to new challenges. Training all summer to make a hockey team. Finding the courage and confidence to effectively chair a Faculty Council meeting of established scholars early in my career. Delivering a conference presentation to a group of content experts. Assuming senior administrator roles early in my career. These are just a few examples of assignments and experiences that stretched me and gave me a platform from which to leap into bigger opportunities. Some assignments were made easier because they extended my previous experience. Others were very new areas for growth and development. At times I questioned whether I had the skills and background to bring them to a successful conclusion. However, perseverance, coaching from others, and guidance helped get me through these challenging times, and upon reflection, these were the experiences from which I gained the most.

> You will find that you tend to value things more if you had to break a sweat to get them.
> —MATTHEW MCCONAUGHEY

Researchers[45] have confirmed that stretch assignments accompanied by deep reflection on the experience, the outcomes, and the key learning points are critical to heightened leader development. Reflection on the strategies, the outcomes, and the learning gleaned from the experience is critical. The experience can also serve as a springboard for developing leaders who now have the experience, confidence, and track record of success to assume other challenging opportunities.

The take home point is to "embrace opportunity." Don't expect to be 100% qualified for every assignment. Have confidence in your abilities and your capacity to learn. Many times, you will learn as you go along. I have found that many of my former female students and graduates often fall prey to this trap. I encourage them, and the male students in my influence also need to encourage the females to think big and go after things. I encourage all of my students not to disqualify themselves. I remind them that the person who eventually assumes the role will undoubtedly have areas that they will need to develop as they undertake the responsibilities.

> If somebody offers you an amazing opportunity, but you are not sure, you can do it, say yes – then learn how to do it later!"
> —RICHARD BRANSON

This philosophy helps explain why I have been a life-long advocate for experiential learning in our institutions of higher learning. I had the honour of creating the first co-operative education program at the University of Windsor and watched first-hand how students grew and developed through this form of education. They were encouraged to accept new challenges, expand their horizons, and enrich their knowledge gained in the classroom with an applied learning experience. Placements were governed and evaluated on the basis of pre-determined learning objectives. All evaluations were linked to these objectives. Realized outcomes were measured against them as well. Finally, and most importantly, the cooperative professionals saw themselves as partners in the education of the student, not as employers. I saw incredible growth in these students as they assumed roles that they might not have been prepared for upon entry. Their skill set grew as did their confidence.

That experiential learning experience helped prepare me to lead a larger Faculty at Western University, where the programs in nursing, physical therapy, occupational therapy, audiology, and speech-language pathology required clinical experiences. My earlier experiences in experiential learning helped me earn this role, and in it, I watched students grow as professionals through their clinical experiences.

I also had the opportunity to watch students grow through international exchange programs. These programs ranged in length from six months to a full year. Exchange students needed to leave the comforts and security of their homes and university and move to another country and take their term or academic year at a partner university. I stayed in contact with many of these students when they were on these exchanges and followed up with them when they returned to join them in reflection activities on the experience. As a Dean and academic leader, I would encounter many of these students years later at alumni events. Invariably, these successful alumni would point to their international exchange experience as a pivotable growth experience that significantly accelerated their development.

## THE NEW PROFESSOR

I began my academic career as a 26 year-old professor of sport management at the University of Regina in 1984. I was excited to be offered this position and embark on my career. I was going to be working with a senior professor and together we were going to develop and deliver this exciting program.

I arrived in late June ahead of my July 1st appointment and immediately headed to the senior professor's office to tell him how excited I was to have the opportunity to work with him. He proceeded to tell me that he was on his way to Europe for a 12-month sabbatical. I needed to develop and deliver the program myself. This certainly qualified as a stretch assignment.

I immediately called my mentors who sent me sample course outlines and program briefs, and before long, the program was developed. I worked hard to deliver the courses and this program was launched. I wasn't much older than the majority of students in my classes, and in fact a number were older than me. I persevered and built on the experience. For the record, it is a highly successful program today at the University of Regina and I am proud to have a played a role in getting it started.

I have often reflected on that experience and learned first-hand how important it is to have trusted mentors who can guide you. I also learned to trust my abilities and to embrace challenges placed before me, and to believe in my ability to take on this challenging assignment. I often reflect on that inauspicious start, and with fondness suggest that it helped prepare me for future challenges that lay ahead.

The same can be said for the first job that students take upon graduation. I have always counselled students to consider the learning and professional development opportunities when making their decisions about their first job. I remind them that it only their first job and they should be mindful of the fact that if they work hard, grow, and prepare effectively, advanced opportunities will follow. Learning and growth opportunities far outweigh salary and benefits at this early stage in their careers. I advise them to do their research and give special consideration to the background, leadership style, and experience of their immediate supervisor. Will this person challenge them and help them learn and grow? Will they provide stretch opportunities for growth? Will they invest in their personal and professional development? Consistent with the research literature[46], I also encourage graduates to consider roles that will provide them with professional growth, expose them to learning opportunities across many areas, and help them develop their skills in working with people. Many people I know (including myself) have taken lower-paying positions that align more with their career ambitions and/or offer them advanced development opportunities that will significantly help them down the road as their career unfolds. Those seeking future leadership roles are encouraged to seek positions that allow them to hone and develop their emotional intelligence skills.

> Colleagues with high leadership potential need to be developed. Organizations that do this well deepen their leadership talent pool by strategically selecting, developing, managing, and mentoring new colleagues as a part of their talent management process.[47]

Uncertainty and challenge must be welcomed and embraced. I encourage my graduates to take calculated risks at this point in their careers because I am convinced that the payoff to their growth and development will pay handsome dividends to them in the future. Leader development expert David Day and his colleagues would wholeheartedly agree.[48]

> People are more likely to grow into leaders when they are in situations that perfectly balance challenge and support.

## FIND ROLE MODELS, MENTORS AND SPONSORS

Research evidence [49] is mounting about the undeniable impact that role models, mentors, and sponsors have on leader development and career development. I have certainly benefited from key individuals who fulfilled these roles in my life. My guess is that upon reflection, readers will also agree that there have been people who have played these roles and facilitated their development as a leader and helped advance their careers. The same person may have filled any one of the three roles over the course of their engagement with you as an aspiring leader. Let's explore these three concepts and differentiate between the three critical roles.

Role models are people we wish to emulate. These people exhibit admirable qualities and behaviors that we admire and respect. We may or may not know our role models personally, and we may have a number of different role models whom we admire for different reasons. Regardless of who the role model might be, research evidence from the *Centre for Leadership & Strategic Thinking* out of the University of Washington confirms that leadership behaviours can be learned and refined through the observation of others.[50] Similar findings were garnered from a study of young doctors[51] who highlighted the impact that their role models had on their development. They believe that they learned professional behaviours, respect for patients, and the importance of integrity by watching senior doctors carry out their duties. They also suggested that the role models they respected the most socialized more, willingly shared their perspectives with the younger doctors, and displayed a positive, optimistic attitude toward their lives and careers. They led by example and inspired the young doctors who felt that these respected physicians cared about them and their development.

Role models can have significant impacts on others at all stages of life. At an early stage, the role model is often played by a parent, a teacher, a community leader, or a coach. Positive role models at this early stage often teach and demonstrate socially acceptable behaviors and ethics that help young people understand how to engage with others and function in the world.[52] Children often learn lessons in empathy, compassion, respect, and tolerance by watching their role models in action. These researchers also noted that children could learn the flip side of these attributes if the role models they respect display negative and unethical behaviours.

My mother was an early role model for me. She was a strong advocate for my brother and me and made many sacrifices for us. She went back to school when we were in high school and became a hairdresser and business owner. Her work ethic and commitment to her customers were well-known and admired by many, including me. I watched her with awe and admiration. She was my hero and role model. Another role model for me was my high school physical education teacher. I admired how he carried himself. He displayed patience and grace. I thought that he had the coolest job on earth, and I wanted to follow in his footsteps. I actually set out to prepare myself as a high school physical education teacher until I encountered other role models who inspired me to pursue another career ambition. When I entered university, I met a number of university professors whom I admired, and I altered my career plans and wanted to follow in their footsteps. In the early stages of my career, I found myself emulating their teaching and research practices. I respected them and found that their behaviours translated well for me. With time, I added my own wrinkles to their approach, but without question, these professors, who later became colleagues, served as career role models for me and emulating them significantly fueled and facilitated my career development. Researchers[53] have concluded that role models and mentors can be especially effective in the career development process for women.

The late Dr. Bob Boucher from the University of Windsor served as an example of a professional role model whom I got to know well and always respected. Bob first captured my attention when I was an undergraduate student in one of his classes. His lectures were exceptionally well organized and professionally delivered. He told great stories and also concluded them with a lesson that could be learned from the experience. He inspired me, and I wanted to be just like him.

Due to his incredible influence, I decided to study in the same area (leadership) as Bob. He agreed to take me on as a graduate sport management advisee (his first), and I wrote a Masters degree thesis in the area of emergent leadership. I travelled with him to conferences and listened to his keynote addresses. I followed his path to a Ph.D. degree at The Ohio State University. I later followed his career path and became a professor and academic leader at the University of Windsor. Bob was a role model who significantly impacted my leader development through his example. However, aspiring leaders need more than role models to develop effectively. They also need mentors and sponsors. Consistent with the literature, the same person can fulfil any, and sometimes all three roles. Bob also served as a mentor and sponsor for me.

Some role models like those noted above are known personally. We may not know other people we consider to be role models, but we are impacted by watching and learning from them. Barack Obama fits that description for me. While I don't know him personally, I admire his character, his vision, his leadership, and his determination. I read books about him with keen interest. I am especially enamored by his exceptional oratory skills. I watch YouTube videos of his speeches and marvel at his command of the language and the efficacy of his delivery. I watch his speeches and find myself "hanging on his every word." I try to emulate the flair and effectiveness that he always displays. He is an example of a role model whom I don't know personally who influenced me, and through his words and actions, helped shape me as a leader.

Looking to quickly access and benefit from years of experience and professional knowledge? Linking with a mentor who is a senior colleague has been proven to be one of the fastest and most effective ways of developing young or less-experienced professionals. Mentorship is an efficient and effective way of helping less experienced colleagues adapt and advance and should be part of a talent development program. However, to get the most of the experience (i.e., for mentees, mentors, and the host organization), there must be trust between the mentor and mentee, and all parties must be committed to making the experience a success.

Mentors are people we personally know, and they provide specific guidance and direction to aspiring leaders. They are usually in the same profession or situation and have great experience, wisdom, maturity, and insights that they can share to help aspiring leaders learn and be more effective. They invest in the aspiring leader and take

## AUTHOR EXPERIENCE – FORMATIVE YEARS

Growing up in a small town provided the author with unlimited opportunities to see my parents, and the parents of my friends lead teams and organizations. My father was a local car dealer. My paternal grandfather and a number of my uncles held political offices. I marvelled at the way these people "worked rooms" and captured the attention of people they encountered. However, my mother had the most impact on my leadership development. She was a small business owner and operator whose beauty salon was the gathering place in my hometown. Customers and visitors would spend hours in her shop, sharing stories. I listened intently and watched my mother listen and engage others. Contemporary leadership researchers would say that she was deploying emotional intelligence, and she was. As is the case with most mothers, she also instilled a confidence and support system that encouraged me to think big and work hard to achieve my dreams.

I later came under the influence of an inspiring physical education teacher in my hometown school by the name of Bob North, and my career path was immediately forged. He was a role model to me. I wanted to be just like him when I "grew up." He had a special influence on me and I modelled his approach to inspiring others and his communication patterns at every opportunity.

These role models had a significant impact on my life during my formative years.

pride in their development. Bob did this for me. I scheduled sessions with him where he would ask me questions about my teaching, research, and administrative roles. I would ask him questions knowing that he would provide me with the best information he could and offer insights that might be helpful. He had my best interests at heart. I could share anything with him knowing that his word was his bond, and I could count on him keeping things we discussed between us. At times we would deconstruct situations and decisions that I made. Where appropriate, he would compliment me on decisions that I made, and, when necessary, suggest alternative courses of action when the results of my decisions were less than ideal. Mentors like this can help mentees advance their skill sets and careers. Researchers have confirmed that effective mentoring programs can also lead to many positive outcomes, including, but not limited to, decreased employee absenteeism, heightened engagement, less turnover, and less likelihood of careers prematurely plateauing.[54]

Some researchers[55] have suggested that effective mentoring can result in benefits to all parties involved in the process.

> Mentoring offers benefits to both mentors, and the mentees, including increased professional skills, decreased stress and anxiety, improved insight, greater awareness, and improved self-esteem.[56]

The benefits to the mentee are undoubtedly the most obvious. Mentees' integration and performance improve more expeditiously. Research has confirmed that they often receive faster promotions, demonstrate leadership behaviours earlier, have more career opportunities, and are generally more satisfied with their careers compared to colleagues who did not have a mentor.[57] I am well aware of the benefits I accrued from the mentors in my life. They accelerated my learning, advanced my integration into higher education, and heightened my confidence levels. They helped put me on the right track and ensured that I stayed on it through their coaching and direction. As an academic leader, I was acutely aware of the benefits and implemented formal mentorship programs with new academic leaders and professors. I remained cognizant of the research results that confirmed that "junior faculty with mentors publish more articles, feel more confident in their capabilities, and are more satisfied overall with their career than those without mentors."[58] This impact was especially true for new female faculty academics and academic leaders. Other researchers[59] have confirmed that career and psychosocial support offered by effective mentors are invaluable contributors to leadership development in mentees. Mentees effectively coach these prospective leaders and provide them with the guidance, insights, and information that they have garnered, given their advanced level of experience. They serve as a sounding board for mentees who can share ideas and possible solutions and get feedback on the approach from their mentor. Effective mentors help their mentees develop their instincts and refine their leadership practices while building skill and confidence along the way. However, while mentees may be the prime beneficiary, they are not the only benefactors. This is not a one-way benefit. Mentors can also benefit and be invigorated from the experience. Many mentors report a higher level of job satisfaction and commitment to the organization, knowing that the host organization trusts them to help develop the next generation of leaders. They often report gains in intrinsic satisfaction. They can also learn new skills and perspectives from mentees who have had different life and career experiences and often different skill sets (e.g., technology). Many of my graduate students have helped me better understand students and their learning styles. Many graduate students have helped me understand technology and how to maximize my use of new gadgets and computer programs. I have learned a great deal from them, and I hope they will say the same about me. Mentors can also gain from participating in the mentoring relationship.

Last but not least, the host organization also benefits from having formal and informal mentoring programs. These benefits include, but are not limited to, enhanced recruitment of talent, faster integration and return on investment, heightened member engagement and commitment, and a more strategic and effective leader succession process.[60] New colleagues can be attracted to organizations that tangibly demonstrate that they are committed to the success of their new hires. Colleagues may decide to stay with organizations longer if they are continuing to develop due to the information, time, and attention that mentors and the organization are investing in them. The organization can also benefit from the advanced skills and confidence levels that employees gain through the mentoring process. What organization doesn't want these outcomes?

Some researchers suggest that an effective mentoring program should follow a sequential pattern.[61] The first stage, labelled the initiation stage, underscores the need for the mentor and mentee to respect and trust each other. Investment, and consequently, the results will be less than what is possible if one party does not respect and trust the other participant. It is also critical that the organization be fully committed to the mentorship program.

Mentoring programs can be formal (i.e., the organization takes responsibility for assigning the mentee to a more experienced mentor who is charged with helping the less experienced colleague adapt and grow). These relationships can be effective if there is mutual trust, respect, and investment. The mentor and mentee must have a compatible relationship. Mentors may require some training and development to maximize their impact, and organizations would be well served in ensuring that they receive this training. Mentors and mentees also need to have time in their workdays devoted to this process and use technological advancements (e.g., teleconferencing) to alleviate the need for extensive travel. If any of these elements are missing, the mentoring experience will undoubtedly fail. Organizations are clearly committed to the process if they take the initiative to implement the formal mentoring program. This is critical to the success of the process.

> Mentors teach how to embrace the struggle – that the struggle is the good part.[62]

Other mentoring relations are informal and more organic. In these situations, a mentee seeks out a more experienced colleague whom they respect, and they both agree to participate in a mentoring relationship. This relationship is often more successful because trust, respect, and investment between the two are usually established in advance. Some research has confirmed that mentees and mentors have more frequent engagement and communications in informal arrangements compared to formal mentor relationships. Regardless of the formal or informal arrangement, the impact of the relationship becomes more impactful when the host organization supports the process (through words of encouragement, ensuring mentors and mentors are provided with the time and resources necessary to help ensure a successful outcome). However, finding a mentor may be challenging. Some female mentees report that they find it especially hard to secure an informal mentor[63], and as a result, may benefit from organizations having a formal mentorship program established by the host organization.

Once trust and respect are assured, cultivation is the next stage of the mentoring process. At this stage, mentors and mentees agree upon the focus of the mentoring relationship (e.g., career progress, skill acquisition). Both parties agree on the content and check in with each other on a regular basis for deep discussions and future planning. Hopefully, competence and confidence will be gained as the parties move through this process. With time, the mentee will become more skilled and experienced and will require less skill advice (but perhaps more career progression mentoring is taking place at this stage). The formal mentoring process could end at this stage, but these researchers suggest that the mentor and mentee can redefine the relations to advance mutual needs.

> Mentoring is an unselfish process. It is altruistic. It is interpersonal. It is a voluntary pairing of two individuals for mutual personal and corporate gain. Mentoring affects many aspects of organizational behavior including leadership, organizational culture, job satisfaction, and performance.[64]

The final area in this critical development piece is the area of sponsorship. Sponsors open up doors of opportunity for aspiring leaders. They advocate for the protégé and use their influence and reputation to advance the careers of their protégé, especially within a field and, most of all, within an organization. Research has proven that both mentorship and sponsorship work well together in preparing and advancing individuals in an organization, leading to reduced levels of turnover and higher levels of employee commitment and satisfaction.[65] Critics might suggest that sponsorship is a form of nepotism, and it could be if unqualified colleagues are advanced through this process. Sponsorship should be something that all qualified colleagues receive. It can be especially helpful in advancing the careers of equity-deserving groups, and organizations and leaders must always ensure that the principles of equity, diversity, and inclusion are respected in any leadership development program. Researchers[66] have found that role models, mentors, and sponsors can be especially effective in propelling women into leadership roles.

Sponsors are experienced colleagues in their field who are respected for their career success, perspectives, and insights. They use this influence to help advance their protégé. Sponsors put their reputations on the line by speaking favourably about aspiring leaders. They encourage others to bring them into their circle. They create opportunities for their protégé because they believe in the person and are willing to put their reputation on the line as a show of support. They effectively open doors of opportunity. Bob Boucher also served as a sponsor for me. He served as a reference for me for job opportunities. He brought my candidacy to the attention of hiring boards. He did what he could to help me advance in my career. I had other people who served in this capacity for me. My former hockey coach and professor, Dr. Bob Corran tirelessly advocated for me as I broke into higher education. I swear that the Dean of the Faculty of Physical Activity Studies at the University of Regina agreed to hire me so he would not have to accept daily phone calls from my sponsor, Dr. Bob Corran.

Some organizations have implemented sponsorship programs

to complement mentoring programs and significantly accelerate the career advancement of young people, and especially those in under-represented ranks. The "Breakthrough Program" launched by Pricewaterhouse Coopers (PwC) is an example of such a program.[67] This program creates opportunities for talented, mid-career women and gives them the preparation and levers to advance to more senior leadership roles. The program was a smashing success. Women advanced into senior leadership roles at a faster rate and were well-prepared for success as a result of the program. Mentors, sponsors, and participants in the program "… learned to be inclusive in decision-making, resourced their leadership teams differently, and thus became agents of change in the organization, and advocates for diversity in leadership positions".[68] The women participating in this program reported that they were more confident, more likely to take risks, and twice as likely to move into senior leadership roles as a result of their participation in this program. This is critical for women because research confirms that men generally have more mentorship and sponsorship opportunities than women (due to a number of factors, including: the prevalence of more men in positions to serve as mentors and sponsors; homogenous reproduction, and; the Queen Bee Syndrome where women who could serve as mentors or sponsors are especially tough on other women). Formal mentorship and sponsorship programs have been effective in breaking this cycle for women.

Researchers have uncovered similar findings for programs targeted to people of colour. Participants in the sponsorship program set up in educational settings found that participants gained greater access to professional networks, access to previously unattainable resources, a greater sharing of information previously withheld from these colleagues, and access to channels that helped them navigate an organization's bureaucracy.[69] Colleagues who have benefitted from mentors and sponsors report higher confidence levels and trust in their abilities. They seek and seize greater assignments and will take risks knowing that their mentor and/or sponsor has their back and can be counted on for support and guidance if needed.

Organizations that want to improve culture, strategy, engagement, and the bottom line will benefit most from investing in improving leadership at all levels. This can begin with identifying employees who naturally possess leadership potential.[70]

Mentors and sponsors invest in their protégé and are invaluable to their development and advancement. I have told mine that I will repay them by doing the exact same for aspiring leaders who I have encountered. I believe that we all have a professional obligation to reward our mentors and sponsors by "throwing the ladder down" and mentoring and sponsoring the next generation of leaders who will hopefully repeat the pattern and keep the circle of influence whole.

While mentors help motivate people to move toward their ultimate goals, sponsors enable them to attain them.[71]

## NEVER STOP LEARNING

Leaders need working knowledge in a variety of areas related to their field or industry. Seek breadth and depth in learning experiences. Unfortunately, some people shy away from opportunities to learn and grow, especially those that are challenging. They can be time consuming and difficult but consider these opportunities as investments in yourself.

Everything that scares you is bravery training !!!
—ROBIN SHARMA

As noted, I started my career as a 26-year old professor at the University of Regina. It was a great opportunity that challenged me and helped prepare me for a role at the University of Windsor that came available. The University of Windsor was looking at adding a colleague who could teach sport management and lead the Campus

Recreation program (and I had two years of valuable experience doing exactly these two things at the University of Regina). However, the Windsor role also called on me to develop and implement a Cooperative Education Program, the first of its kind at the University of Windsor.

While I valued experiential learning, I knew nothing about co-operative education and needed to prepare myself for my interview. I knew that I needed to gain insights and experience to secure the role. I was convinced that it could be a steppingstone in my leadership and career advancement. I talked with industry leaders in the field and gained their insights into the keys for success. I read voraciously about the area. After I assumed the role, I immediately spent time on the campus of the University of Waterloo, arguably the university in Canada with the strongest record in cooperative education, to learn more about the area. The Co-operative Education Program in the Faculty of Human Kinetics was then launched and subsequently served as the springboard for co-operative education programs in other academic areas on the Windsor campus. As anticipated, that role was fundamental to my development. The learning I garnered in experiential learning gave me the experience and administrative support to later become the Dean of the Faculty of Human Kinetics at the University of Windsor. That knowledge and experience in decanal leadership and experiential learning subsequently gave me the background that a larger university needed and led to my appointment as the Dean of the Faculty of Health Sciences at Western University. Upon reflection, saying yes to leading an area that was outside my comfort zone and one that required me to gain breadth experience was instrumental to my career advancement in academic leadership.

Think about your career and leadership aspirations and the skill sets that might be important for your development and your experience profile. Join task force committees where you will gain working knowledge and experience in the area. Say yes to invitations to join volunteer boards and committees that align with your leadership development plans. Reach out to colleagues who agree to serve as your sponsor and open up doors of opportunity for you to get involved on standing and task force committees and on volunteer boards. The fact of the matter is that there are many groups and organizations that need help and would welcome your involvement. My experience also suggests that many standing and task force committees need to work hard to fill their membership. Help them by proactively seeking these opportunities, and in doing so, better prepare yourself for future success in leadership.

Some organizations build job rotation and work teams into their leader development programs. These practices help expose colleagues to a variety of operations and fuel their conceptual development. The Topeka plant of General Foods is one setting that has strategically, and effectively implemented this program. High-potential employees are rotated through a variety of assignments designed to increase the broad skill set of these future leaders. Heightened and faster leader development wasn't the only benefit. Research[72] conducted over a 20-year time frame confirmed that lower employee turnover, less employee absenteeism, and organizational productivity were realized. This finding aligns with other researchers[73] who believe that learning and reflecting while "on the job" and in the natural environment is the most effective method of developing leaders. These researchers believe that leaders can effectively learn leadership skills (i.e., self-management skills, relationship-building skills; management/execution skills, and; cognitive skills) in stretch assignments and other in-house, action learning environments. Colleagues are challenged and engaged in this process. They are charged with reflecting on what they have learned and forced to reflect on how the new skills will help them in future leadership roles. Levels of complexity and learning are advanced as the participants move through the program and are assigned new responsibilities. The participants' competency, confidence, and conceptual skills are developed as they move through the process of experiencing new environments and challenges.

## PARTAKE IN FORMAL LEADER DEVELOPMENT PROGRAMS

Do leadership development programs work? Naturally as a long-time provider of these programs, I subscribe to the belief that they do, especially when accompanied by ongoing, and strategically conceived coaching and mentoring activities. Researchers [74] have studied this area and support my conclusions. However, many are skeptical. A recent survey of 1500 senior managers at 50 organizations underscored the skeptics. Nearly 75% of senior management in this survey were dissatisfied with the learning and development taking place in these 50 organizations. There may be reasons why these senior leaders feel this way (e.g., content not current or customized to the needs of participants, ineffective design or delivery of the program, lack of commitment from participants, lack of support from senior leaders or their organization, no ongoing reflection, mentorship, or follow-up). However, I believe leader development programs are critically important and I am especially comforted by the results of the meta-analytical studies [75] that have examined the efficacy of leadership development programs and uncovered promising results. Lacerenza and her colleagues [76] have produced convincing evidence that strategic leader development programs can significantly develop leaders by heightening their knowledge on the topic and developing the skills and judgement necessary to be more effective in the role. Similar results have been realized in leader development programs in military organizations.[77] This leader development model (known as BKD) focuses on three elements, namely, the development of the individual and their character attributes (i.e., Be); their leadership competencies (i.e., Know), and their decision-making abilities (i.e., Do). It is a comprehensive and a conceptually strong program. The "Be" elements include a focus on values, character, discipline, judgement, trust, confidence and self-control. The "Know " portion of the program is focussed on interpersonal, conceptual, and technical skills needed to excel in leadership roles. The "Do" elements of the program include training on influencing others, setting goals, inspiring and empowering others, aligning resources and strategy, developing others, and ensuring a positive learning culture. Leaders of the program look for incremental gains in participants, and research[78] has demonstrated that it works.

In my view, leader development programs must be ongoing. We expect far too much from the single-shot seminars or the two-day weekend leader development sessions. Leader development experts often refer to this process as the "spray and pray" approach where colleagues attend a weekend seminar, hear a number of presentations, and return to their host organization a day or two later with hopes that they will be a better leader. We know that this is never the case. Leader development programs must be ongoing. Content must be conceptually conceived and specifically aligned with the needs of the participants. One size does not fit all situations or cultures. Effective leader development must include opportunities for reflection, for trial and error, and for situation deconstruction with a qualified coach and mentor. Leaders must remain a work in progress. They have to stay current on trend and topic areas in their field as well as within the area of leadership.

## "GET YOUR TICKET PUNCHED"

Richard Peddie has been a professional mentor of mine for many years. Richard held the title of President and CEO of Maple Leaf Sports and Entertainment, arguably the most powerful, and influential sport leadership role in Canada. In addition to his professional role, Richard is a leadership enthusiast and author of two leadership books. I have spent a considerable amount of time with Richard over the years and turned to him for guidance and advice. I also had him speak to my leadership classes and offer my undergraduate and graduate students advice on their career planning and leader development. Richard would always tell them to "get their ticket punched", and share his story.

Richard enjoyed the sport of basketball and as a young student at the University of Windsor he would watch the Windsor Lancer Basketball team and dream of a career running a professional basketball franchise. His dream never faded. However, as he eloquently shared with my students, he needed to get experience in the key areas so he could qualify for an interview and fulfill his dream. He strategically, and successfully built his career foundation and made his dream a reality. He built his career in the key areas of senior sport leadership. He pursued roles based on the knowledge and experience he would acquire. He studied the industry and knew he would need experience in areas like facility management, food and beverage, and broadcasting and telecommunications. He sought senior leadership positions in each of these industries.

When the Toronto Maple Leafs and Toronto Raptors teams came under one ownership group, Richard "had his ticket punched" in all the key areas, and subsequently, became a natural choice as the founding President and CEO of Maple Leaf Sports and Entertainment. His example is exhibit A of the role that sterling testimony of a leader strategically building a career in leadership by acquiring the breadth and depth experiences needed to qualify, and later excel in an industry.

Thanks Richard.

Organizational leaders who stage the one day seminars, and are often, and predictably disappointed with the results, soon begin to question the investment. Sometimes these decision-makers become cynical about investing in leader development programs. This shouldn't be the case. Truly effective leader development programs are ongoing. They are spaced out over a period of time with opportunities for reflection, 1-1 discussions, small group activities, readings, and opportunities to practice. They include and integrate ongoing coaching and mentorship.

For example, the academic leader development program (i.e., Western Leader Academy) that I lead on my campus is an example of a program that incorporates the latest advancements in leader development. Over the course of the year-long program, participants who have been nominated by their units, are exposed to the theoretical development in both academic management and leadership. Content for the program is developed after surveying the participants, determining their needs, and ensuring that the content aligns with their needs and the current and emerging issues facing contemporary higher education leaders.

> "All the best practice firms report having specialized, highly customized, "by nomination only" leadership development programs for their high potential employees. These programs typically involve a heavy commitment by senior executives in the sponsorship and delivery of the program, often supplemented by facilitation and coaching by outside specialists."[79]

Participants in the Western Leader Academy program also engage in case study activities and role playing situations designed to imbed learning and content transfer. We deconstruct current events in higher education, the decisions that were rendered at the time, and the decisions we might make as leaders in that situation given the realized outcomes and the benefits of time and reflection. Readings are carefully selected, assigned and deconstructed. Participants are engaged throughout the year-long program in small group activities and have 1-1 coaching opportunities with me. We complete diagnostic measures to help me better understand individual areas of strength and areas for development. Special emphasis is given to developing the participants' levels of emotional intelligence given its pivotal role in academic leader success. I bring content experts and experienced academic leaders into the Academy to speak on topics that fall outside of my area of expertise. I continue to have regular contact with participants and engage in leadership coaching, mentoring and sponsorship long after the formal program has concluded. This program aligns perfectly with the developments in the leader development research base.

I am proud of Western University and its commitment to leader development. The Western Leader Academy, which I lead, is exactly the type of leader development program that prepares leaders of the future and gives people the content, contacts, and courage to assume academic leadership roles, and succeed in them once secured. I am honoured to be leading that initiative and encourage organizations, and their leaders, both in and outside higher education, to be more strategic and proactive in leader development initiatives. An overview of the Western Leader Academy Program is presented in Appendix A.

> Leadership, like swimming, cannot be learned by reading about it.
>
> —HENRY MINTZBERG

Leaders can be developed, but one size does not fit all participants. Their needs must be determined in advance. Content must be current and reflect the current and future needs of participants. Leadership assessments can be helpful as can surveys of participants' strengths, areas of challenge, and career aspirations. Getting 360 feedback can be especially helpful in assessing the needs of participants. Time must be invested in these individuals through ongoing coaching and mentoring interventions. One shot seminars and workshops are rarely, if ever effective.

Researchers[80] who have weighed in on the future of leadership development highlight the need for customized training and development and the need for conceptually strong leader development programs. Technology allows for more interactions between the facilitator and the participant and the digitization of content will accommodate participants learning at their own pace given their other responsibilities. They suggest more in-house, on the job learning will be the wave of the future, with facilitators helping learners deconstruct situations and decisions and reflect on the leadership learning.

Coaches and consultants doing leadership development today are often engaging the entire leadership team in a series of development activities designed to make the leadership team more effective. This is a less popular format of leadership development, but one that is important given the premium contemporary leadership consultants and theorists place on a team approach to leadership. I expect this type of leader development program to continue in the years ahead.

## HAVE THE CONFIDENCE TO LEAD, HAVE A PLAN, AND REFLECT ON THE RESULTS

Can one develop the requisite skills and experiences needed to assume leadership roles in the future should they decide to pursue these opportunities? Absolutely. As noted in this section of the book, leaders can be developed. Engage in group activities. Seek learning opportunities that will strengthen and broaden your knowledge base. Take leader development programs, and especially those that develop and refine your emotional intelligence skills. Seek out role models and emulate the behaviours and leadership practices that align with your skill set and values. Secure trusted and respected mentors and sponsors who can facilitate your growth and open doors of opportunity for you. Take the initiative to lead smaller units or projects to develop and refine your leadership skills and give you the experience and confidence needed to assume larger leadership roles in the future. Finally, take the time to periodically assess your impact, the results of some of your leadership practices and decisions, and your ongoing leadership development. This can be done quarterly, biannually, and at a minimum, annually. Self and other leadership diagnostic data can help you identify areas of strength as well as signal areas in need of future development. Take the time to think and reflect on your practices and progress. Keep a journal and record honest self-assessments to questions like:

1. Am I looking after myself? My family, my career, and my friends?
2. What do I need to keep doing? What areas need more attention?
3. What activities will I commit to over the next review period to improve in each of these areas?

In the end, I counsel current and future leaders to be confident in themselves, in their skill sets and experiences, and in their futures. You won't have to have all the answers, and in fact, the best leaders are comfortable with vulnerability, messiness, and an awareness that others may have better answers to the questions and challenges that confront us. Trust them, and yourself. Followers value leaders who respect and engage others. Be daring, confident and trusting of yourself and of others (unless proven otherwise). Naturally, there will be bumps along the journey, but with a clear focus and a strong team, effective leaders will eventually prevail. Expect criticism as it goes with the leadership role. However, be mindful of the perspective of Deebo Swinney, the Head Football coach at Clemson University who advised leaders to not worry about criticism for people from whom you wouldn't seek advice. Consider the source. Some people like to complain and be critical, often due to their own insecurities.

You may also take comfort in the words of F. Scott Fitzgerald who noted that,

> For what it's worth... it's never too late, or in my case too early, to be whoever you want to be. There's no time limit. Start whenever you want. You can change or stay the same. There are no rules to this thing. We can make the best or the worst of it. I hope you make the best of it. I hope you see things that startle you. I hope you feel things you've never felt before. I hope you meet people who have a different point of view. I hope you live a life you're proud of, and if you're not, I hope you have the courage to start over again.

## AN ACTIVITY: MY LIFE NOW AND IN 20 YEARS

I have my undergraduate and graduate students engage in a private visioning session designed to map out their lives and leadership plans (personal and professional) over the next 20 years. I encourage them to be creative, to consider their values and determine what is truly important to them. I ask them to put no constraints on their plans, and remind them that with work and investment that they can be and do virtually anything they set their minds and heart to do. I ask them to not put constraints on their plans at this point in the process and to not worry about what others will think about their plans as no one else will see them. Once completed, I ask them to reflect on this end and how they feel about it. If they like it they are then encouraged to map out a route to get there (think of Richard Peddie's quest to lead a professional basketball team). To help the students I will usually map out the plan that I set at age 26 to becoming a Dean (e.g., obtaining the right education, developing the necessary skill set, securing trusted mentors and sponsors along the way, and garnering the necessary experiences that would qualify for the Decanal opportunity when it became available). I am clear about the success milestones and honest about the setbacks that I encountered on the journey.

I have found this exercise to be helpful in giving students a road map to realizing their dreams. Too many take life as it comes, with no plans. That is fine if this is what is important to them. I have had students tell me that their future aim is to be happy and have sufficient resources to live a comfortable family-oriented life … and I applaud this aim. Others seek to be the Prime Minister which I equally applaud.

I only ask that students be authentic, true to their identified values, confident, and thoughtful in the exercise. I close the activity by reciting my favorite John Lennon quote that puts everything in perspective for me and the students and reinforces the need for them to be confident.

> Everything will be OK in the end, and if it's not OK,
> it's not the end.
>
> —JOHN LENNON

## SUMMARY

The question of whether leaders are born or made is as old as the study of leadership itself. Research has confirmed that both elements play a role and degree can vary based on family dynamics and other factors. I believe that opportunity and a desire to lead are also important considerations in understanding who emerges into leadership roles and who doesn't. This literature was discussed in this section of the book.

That said, readers have been provided with an overview of the key areas that have been proven to be essential to leader development at key stages in life. Key opportunities for leader development were presented for the early years, the adolescent years, and the higher education years. However, as noted in this section of the book, leadership learning can and must, take place at all stages of life if leaders are going to emerge and be effective in the leadership role. We can always learn and we must always be learning. Things change, and leaders who aren't continually growing will find that their influence fades expeditiously. As noted in that portion of the book, a commitment to lifelong learning is required.

> Don't be afraid of the space between your dreams and reality. If you can dream it, you can make it so.
> — BELVA DAVIS

Those aspiring to leadership roles would be well served in studying and bolstering their levels of emotional intelligence. I believe that it is the single most important factor in determining leadership emergence and success in the role. The comforting fact is that emotional intelligence can be learned. Readers are informed of the research advances and strategies for developing the three critical areas of emotional intelligence, namely, their (a) self-awareness; (b) self-management, and; (c) empathy. They are also informed of the importance of developing their skills in reflection and how important that skill is to leader development and success. The section concludes with a plan for leader development and why aspiring leaders need to pursue growth opportunities, especially early in their lives and careers, how role models, mentors, and sponsors facilitate leader development and success, and how formal leader development programs can facilitate tremendous growth and prosperity for current and aspiring leaders.

> Human nature is the most important thing to understand if you're a leader
>
> —TEDDY ROOSEVELT

This part of the book focused on leader development and how to get on the leadership lifecycle flywheel. The following section provides insights and six critical leadership practices that leaders should adopt to excel in the leadership role.

> You are destined to become the person you decide to be.
>
> —RALPH EMERSON WALDO

# THE LAUNCH AND MATURITY PHASE

## A READER'S GUIDE:

Upon reading this section, readers will understand that:

- ○ leadership truly is a "team sport";
- ○ there are six essential leadership practices that leaders should implement and refine to maximize their effectiveness;
- ○ getting off to a good start is critical. There is a science and art to ensuring this happens.
- ○ honest, forward-thinking leaders who empower and inspire others and ensure their ongoing growth can attract and retain the very best talent on their leadership teams. Building and inspiring great teams is critical to leadership success;
- ○ leaders are often evaluated on their ability to exercise good judgement and make good decisions. Leaders can heighten their abilities in these areas;

○ ensuring clarity and focus for a group or organization is a key leadership responsibility.

○ the best leaders engage, inspire, and motivate, and;

○ top leaders are progressive, forward-looking, always learning, and inspiring others to do the same.

Congratulations. You have made it. You have prepared yourself by using some or all of the suggestions outlined earlier in this book and you have now emerged as the formal leader of your unit or organization. People now look to you for leadership.

Leadership can be one of the most rewarding aspects of your career. Watching colleagues develop and excel in their careers and the group you are leading is very rewarding. However, there will be difficult times. People will disappointment you. You will face daunting challenges and encounter challenging times. Expect both the good and the bad, knowing:

> Rough seas make stronger sailors. Tough times build greater people.
>
> —ROBIN SHARMA

This section of the book has been prepared to help leaders effectively and successfully navigate these waters of uncertainty, increase the likelihood of the good times, and hopefully minimize the challenging situations. Leaders can do things to significantly heighten their impact. They can also do things to derail their efficacy. My hope is that this chapter will help leaders discover what they can do to maximize the former outcomes and minimize the later scenarios. While it is prepared from the context of organizational leadership, it is important to reemphasize that leadership is not a role or position (although our hope is that those in positions of influence effectively lead). We all know of many examples of strong and effective leaders without lofty titles, and conversely, we know many examples of people with impressive job titles who are not leaders. Leadership is a social process that is synonymous with influence and helps people or groups individually and collectively attain a desired end. The lessons outlined in this section equally apply to informal leaders who have emerged to influence others.

Leadership has often been described as one of the most studied, yet least understood concepts in the social sciences. Theorists have pursued a number of lines of inquiry, from the early "Great Man" theory of leadership, followed by the behavioural models, to the situational leadership theories, and finally, the transactional and transformational models of leadership. Other scholars have focused on the charismatic attributes of leaders. These theorists have pioneered a greater understanding of leadership, but critics argue that the study and practice of leadership must change with the times. It is safe to assume that the prevalent approaches to leadership and management are outdated, ineffective, and in need of a complete overhaul. The late leadership guru, Warren Bennis agreed, suggesting that it was time to discard the heroic, "larger than life" leader concept. Contemporary leadership experts know that the best leaders are selfless people who are part of the group. They operate best when they adopt a "coaching" paradigm. They assemble, focus, and inspire great teams of leaders who collectively engender higher levels of achievement, and in doing so, transform their organizations into higher functioning units . They genuinely care about those they lead, and they focus and energize colleagues through their words and disciplined actions, not as disengaged individuals who operate from the "command and control" perspective that underscored much of the early theories of leadership.

> If you chase two rabbits you will not catch either one.
> —RUSSIAN PROVERB

## LEADERSHIP IS A TEAM SPORT

As a former hockey player and team sport athlete, coach, and administrator, I have personally experienced the highs and lows of team accomplishment. I have witnessed, with pride and interest, outstanding coaches and team leaders who strategically aligned players and resources, and realized individual and team success. Occasionally, I encountered coaches and players who were less effective in bringing the best out in our teams, leading to disappointing results. However, the experiences, both good and bad, reinforced my perspective, now confirmed in the literature[81], that leadership is a team sport. In fact, the team approach to leadership is ideally suited to leading in the disruptive times that we are in. Contemporary leaders face a host of changes (e.g., technology, post-pandemic economic and social issues, transient workforce, heightened immigration, and environmental realities). In some sectors, like higher education, the demands for information and the challenges of engagement often lead to disputes requiring skillful resolution. A healthy (ideally) discussion and debate are required. Without effective leadership, debates can get personal, petty, and counterproductive. Colleagues that leaders encounter in this day and age seek, if not demand, intellectual stimulation, authentic engagement, and plentiful opportunities for participative governance. Effective leaders need to unleash the creative talents of these members, especially in these times when the need for effective leadership in many sectors may be at an all-time high due to: (a) the social and behavioural impacts of the pandemic; (b) the escalating competition for talent, and (c) the impact of demographic realities in some sectors[82] (e.g., the increase in the number of people entering retirement and the relative decline in the number of younger workers).

The pandemic significantly disrupted society, and its impacts will be significant, long-lasting, and far-reaching. Leaders and their leadership teams may have fewer resources from traditional sources, and opportunities to raise alternative sources of funding could be challenging, if not impossible. Organizations may need to get by with less. They will need to adapt. The need for strong and effective leadership may be more acute than ever to navigate effectively in a post-pandemic environment. There will be a temptation to immediately return to the pre-pandemic management and leadership practices of the past. That may be a mistake. Industries were forced to adapt their work in the digital space, and the system survived. Necessity was once again the "mother of invention." Technological advantages supported alternative means of operation. Meetings and conferences were conducted remotely. Some took the opportunity to question whether some of these meetings were even needed. Effective leaders must continue to be on the lookout for best practices that heighten their impact and effectiveness, as well as that of their units. Technology can facilitate so much more for leaders, but only if they stay up on the technological advancements so they can benefit from its full integration.

Contemporary leaders face immense challenges, and if they are to be successful, they will need to assemble a strong, inspired, and cohesive leadership team that participates actively in unit-wide leadership. Researchers[83] underscore the importance of installing the right people on a leadership team, and readers would be well served reading Cohn and Moran's insightful book[84] entitled: *Why are we so bad at picking good leaders? A better way to evaluate leadership potential.* These authors scoured the leader effectiveness literature and suggested that leaders and/or selection committees need to look for seven attributes in leadership candidates, namely: (a) integrity; (b) empathy; (c) emotional intelligence; (d) vision; (e) judgement; (f) courage, and (g) passion. They provide exceptional examples of how these attributes are blended into the leader behaviours of effective leaders. Securing valid measures of these attributes can be challenging for those charged with making decisions on new leaders, but these authors strongly suggest that decision-makers gather as much information and assessment tools as possible to measure prospective candidates against these attributes (i.e., focused reference checks, psychological assessments, asking candidates to share experiences that might allow decision-makers to test for the presence of these attributes). My colleagues in the Ivey Business School[85] would concur on the importance of character to leader selection and subsequent effectiveness. Do not leave these measures to chance. Leaders and their units would also be well-versed in the principles and legalities of the equity, diversity, and inclusion (EDI) practices. These practices are mandated in many organizations.

In addition to being just and fair, they can also help foster diversity, the production of new ideas and perspectives, and add significant richness to their leadership teams[86]. In addition to being the "right thing to do," strong and effective EDI practices have been shown to make leadership teams stronger and more effective.[87]

> The role of a creative leader is not to have all the ideas;
> it's to create a culture where everyone can have ideas
> and feel that they're valued.
> — SIR KENNETH ROBINSON

Leaders must get on the path to leadership prosperity where they can effectively apply the most recent developments in leadership to heighten their leadership effectiveness and advance their respective units. The six practices outlined below will be especially helpful as leaders thrive in the role.[88]

# SIX ESSENTIAL LEADERSHIP PRACTICES

> Success is simple.
> Do what's right,
> the right way,
> at the right time.
> — ANDREW GLASGOW

## LEADERSHIP PRACTICE #1 – GET OFF TO A GREAT START

Getting off to a great start is critical for leaders entering a new role or situation. A great start can lay the foundation to facilitate future success. Some never recover from a poor start. I have always felt that this was a critically important part of the journey and, as a result, I spent considerable time with incoming leaders to help get them off to a good start.

Do not wait until the conditions are perfect to begin.
Beginning makes the conditions perfect.
— ALAN COHEN

Colleagues brought in from other organizations were always reminded to do all they could to depart from their previous stop on positive terms. I have always been flexible with transition dates as a way of helping colleagues effectively navigate this transition. I reminded colleagues to effectively wrap things up and leave their previous posts with the satisfaction that they saw things through to completion. It was important for them, as it was our organization and me, that incoming colleagues departed their previous stop on good terms. In fact, I believe that how a person leaves a post is just as important as how one starts a new role. Stay to the end, finish challenging projects, deal with problematic issues, and as a final indicator of commitment, be the last person out of the office on your last day.

Rough weather makes good timber.
— JAMES DOBSON RELAYING A
FAMOUS MAINE PROVERB.

Prior to their arrival in our organization, I would often give new leaders program reviews and other information on the role that they were about to assume, as well as a copy of Michael Watkins' insightful book entitled *The First 90 Days – Proven Strategies for Getting Up to Speed Faster and Smarter.*[89] In this book, Watkins highlights the importance of getting up to speed on the group or organization, understanding the brutal facts, the importance of active listening, and the necessity of building trusting relationships with colleagues and other key stakeholders. Everyone is understandably anxious at this transition stage, and it is important for incoming leaders to demonstrate that they listen and they care. Be visible. Meet colleagues in their settings by walking around. Don't make promises that you can't keep or have not clearly thought through. It is better to under-promise and over-deliver at this entry stage. Be sure to follow through on commitments that you do make. Colleagues are especially anxious to see proof that they can trust their new leader. Successfully complete some smaller things, communicate and celebrate the success, credit the contributions of those involved, and build upon these small wins.

Special attention needs to be paid at this stage to building strong, trusting relationships with your leadership team. You can be clear about the expectations you hold for yourself and for others. Be clear about their mandate as well as the support that you will give them to deliver on their mandate. Highlight the team approach that you will bring to the unit and find opportunities to publicly demonstrate your commitment to the team approach to leadership, especially early in your term. Remind colleagues that your approach is a team approach and you count on colleagues raising ideas and perspectives, especially those that run counter to your ideas. Remind them that being part of a leadership team requires them to think about collective success and that they will be counted on to support other leaders on the team. Tell them that you will be happy to make final decisions, if necessary, but in your view, the best approach is always a team approach to decision-making and participative leadership. Once stated, live the concept. Actively mine their ideas. Ask their opinions. Find opportunities to move away from your ideas and support their concepts where appropriate. Once decided, remind colleagues of the importance of sticking together, holding each other accountable for agreed-upon action, and consistently sharing the decision and progress towards its attainment with other colleagues in the organization. Consistency and loyalty are especially important at this stage once decisions are made. Finally, identify some smaller projects and see them through to completion so you can build upon these small wins. Getting off to a great start is critical for leaders. This approach can help ensure that it happens.

The beginning is the most important part of the work.
—PLATO

## LEADERSHIP PRACTICE #2 - BUILD, EMPOWER, AND INSPIRE A FORMIDABLE LEADERSHIP TEAM

Leaders have usually demonstrated the discipline necessary to advance their careers and profiles to a point that they are viewed as credible, accomplished, and respected to assume the leadership role. The skills needed to advance their careers to this point have served them well and qualified them for greater attention and respect from their peers. Their accomplishments may have led them to middle management positions in the industry where they have further demonstrated both managerial and leadership acumen. While some of these skills are transferable to senior leadership roles, new skills and different thinking are also required for senior levels of leadership[90]. Colleague and unit successes are now the critical measures. Effective leaders at the senior levels must be more selfless and now derive their satisfaction from the advancement of the organization and the personal success of their members. Leaders and prospective leaders need to come to this conclusion. Some struggle with this reality and it impairs their effectiveness as a senior leader.

> There are no passengers on Spaceship Earth. We are all crew.
>
> —MARSHALL MCLUHAN

It is clear to me and to other leadership writers of the day that the key to leadership and long-term organizational success is teamwork. Teamwork "... remains the ultimate competitive advantage, both because it is so powerful and so rare"[91], a position that Lencioni[92] intensifies in a later book entitled: *The ideal team player: How to recognize and cultivate three essential virtues.* Leaders need the wisdom, energy, and diverse perspectives of strong and committed team members. As Bill George[93] notes in his "*7 Lessons for Leading in Crisis*" book, leaders cannot do it alone. They must surround themselves with other strong leaders and benefit from their energy, engagement, and contributions.

Leaders who can mine the ideas of other leaders, engage them in joint problem-solving and decision-making and authentically demonstrate that they value their contributions and commitment are on a path to prosperity.

> Always be a first-rate version of yourself instead of a second-rate version of somebody else.
> —JUDY GARLAND

Leaders generally lead units headed by Chairs, Directors, or Vice-Presidents. These individuals must see themselves as part of a team and accept the duality of leadership. They must be held accountable for effectively leading their specific unit <u>and</u> for taking an active role in helping to lead the organization. This facilitates active engagement and development of members, leads to a fuller understanding of issues, and usually, better decision-making. This level of engagement also facilitates heightened organizational clarity and understanding by having members accurately and effectively communicate high-level decisions and their underlying rationale to members in their units. They are true and authentic members of a leadership team. As noted earlier, the higher one rises in an organizational hierarchy, the more complex the situation. Leaders must listen carefully and recognize that there are rarely perfect answers that please everyone. However, this approach usually leads to better decisions.

Leaders need the members of their leadership team to accept this duality of focus. If they are unwilling to adopt this approach, they are clearly the wrong people for the role. Leaders must lay the groundwork for this approach through an honest commitment to transparency and integrity – in the interview and in the leader's day-to-day activities. This helps build trust, pride, and commitment to the larger goals of the organization. In addition to engaging these colleagues and tapping into their expertise, this approach to leadership facilitates their development as leaders. Leaders who adopt this leadership style will also find that they can attract and ignite high-performing leaders to their leadership teams.

> Surround yourself only with people who are going to lift you higher.
>
> —OPRAH WINFREY

Lencioni[94] helps leaders understand the mechanics and benefits of collective leadership. He believes that assembling and deploying a strong, cohesive team is critical to the success of a unit and that this is a leader's most fundamental task. Strong functioning teams usually make better decisions and communicate more effectively. They also foster higher levels of clarity and commitment, especially around issues of purpose and direction. Finally, strong teams are generally comprised of members who are more satisfied, focused, and, ultimately, more effective.

> Simplicity is the ultimate sophistication.
>
> —LEONARDO DA VINCI

Leaders would also be well served by reviewing Daniel Kahneman's[95] insightful book entitled *Thinking, Fast and Slow*. In doing so, they will understand the mistakes people succumb to in the decision-making process (e.g., frequent rush to judgement, engaging in groupthink, and making similar to me errors). Leaders are often judged on the quality of the decisions that they make. Kahneman's practices will help leaders navigate this critical function. Leaders would also benefit from reading the insights captured in Susan Cain's book[96], entitled *Quiet: The power of introverts in a world that cannot stop talking*. Introverts are often overlooked around the meeting table or for leadership positions, yet, as Cain clearly illustrates, they can be a great source of information and/or candidates for leadership roles. Whatever the process, one thing is certain – leaders must get this right. People decisions are the most important decisions that leaders make.

Once assembled, senior leaders must operate like a team. Lencioni's[97] *Five Dysfunctions of a Team* book was required reading for members of my leadership team. Teamwork is ideally suited to contemporary leadership, but it often breaks down and/or operates at less than full capacity. As Lencioni explains, "success comes only for those groups that overcome the all-too-human behavioural tendencies that corrupt teams and breed dysfunctional politics within them."[98] Academic leaders have strong opinions and egos that can get in the way of effective team functioning. At times, and if unchecked, members of a group can selfishly search for what is best for their units at the expense of what is best for the other units and/or organization. Authentic teams adopt the fundamental principle that they will actively participate in shared governance, designed to ensure that the organization and all its units reach their potential. Leaders need to charge their team leaders with the duality of focus, ensuring members:

- effectively lead their respective unit;
- actively participate in the leadership of the organization;
- support and encourage other members of the leadership team, and;
- learn, grow, and enjoy the experience.

Leaders must work to identify, recruit and promote members with this orientation to leadership. Furthermore, members of the leadership team must fill leadership positions in their respective units with people who share this perspective. Adopting this leadership paradigm can lead to these positive transformations.

Lencioni[99] offers suggestions for building and deploying highly functional teams. First of all, he notes that high-functioning teams are comprised of members who trust each other to be open, honest, and supportive. Members must admit when they are wrong. He further suggests that leaders can go a long way to building trust in their teams and establishing this mode of operation when they show their vulnerability and a willingness to change positions or admit when they are wrong. Leaders must lead by example in this area.

## NEW DEAN IN TOWN

In 2004, I had the opportunity to join Western University as the Dean of the Faculty of Health Sciences. It was a large, complex Faculty comprised of five schools and 4500 students. I was currently serving as the Dean of the Faculty of Human Kinetics at the University of Windsor, a much smaller academic unit in a much smaller university.

I had completed two degrees at the University of Windsor, wore the colours of the University as a hockey player, and had an 18-year employment history at the University of Windsor. It was a difficult decision to leave the institution, but one that I needed to make in order to grow as a leader. I ensured that I completed all of the tasks that I needed to complete prior to my July 1, 2004 appointment at Western. True to the advice I continue to give others, I worked in my Windsor office on June 30, 2004, and after walking the hall for the last time as Dean and ensured that I was the last person in the building, I turned the lights off, closed my office door and headed to London.

Western officials conduct an external review of units in advance of a leadership change so I had a detailed report that helped me identify the areas of strength and those in need of attention. The Provost was also crystal clear about the mandate that I would be asked to fulfil. I read as much as I could about the University and Faculty prior to my arrival.

Building a strong and productive culture, heightening research outcomes, and elevating engagement were the top priorities for the new Dean. As a leadership scholar, I knew that culture building and communications were critical to leadership success. I campaigned for the role on the basis on my communications skills.

On the morning of July 1, 2004, I sent out my first Dean's Update, an electronic newsletter that I had used as a communication vehicle at the University of Windsor. I highlighted how excited I was to be joining the Faculty and how much I looked forward to working with everyone in the Western Faculty. I indicated that I looked forward to visiting their academic units in the coming days and spending time with them and hearing about their success stories and areas of challenge. I received a number of notes from colleagues that day who stated that they appreciated me reaching out. Some commented that I was showing them that I was clearly serious about heightening communications – and I was. It was an authenticity test, and one that I appeared to pass. However, I needed to continue to demonstrate my commitment to engagement, culture building, and communications. Subsequently, my newsletter went out every month for the next 11.5 years and it, along with other engagement and communication activities (especially social media vehicles), continues to be the hallmark of my leadership practice.

I finished my last day in the role the same way I started it. I sent out a communication update thanking members for their incredible contributions and reminding them that I would follow their careers and unit progress with incredible pride and interest.

It helps promote a culture of honesty and ownership, attributes that are critical to effective team leadership. Secondly, Lencioni suggests that strong teams enthusiastically and routinely explore ideas. Members must vigorously debate their positions on issues and present cogent arguments that will help move the collective unit forward. They must feel comfort in doing so without anticipating the fear of persecution or ridicule. This has special application for contemporary environments as members are usually intelligent, insightful, and passionate. It is only natural that members have different viewpoints and opinions. Leaders of strong teams welcome contrasting viewpoints because they know that detailed analysis usually leads to better decisions. Leaders can build this approach into their teams by encouraging members to push back their ideas as well as those of other members. Team members will soon welcome the opportunity to have their ideas explored in the spirit of doing what is best for the organization. Lencioni notes that the third barrier to effective team functioning is the lack of closure and commitment to rendered decisions. He says that leaders can quickly and effectively overcome this dysfunction by insisting on closure and a clear and unified course of action once adequate discussion/debate has transpired. Committing action, accountability, and a timeline to paper will assist the team in overcoming key barriers to effective team functioning.

According to Lencioni, the fourth barrier to effective teamwork is the unwillingness of team members to hold other members accountable for following through on actions. Leaders can overcome this barrier by ensuring that the third barrier is covered off, consistently following through on commitments themselves, and calling members out when they do not follow through on commitments (and encouraging all members to do this). This will establish accountability as an operating principle and help make the team highly functional. Members will soon know that meetings, discussions and decisions are taken seriously, and they will be held accountable for action. This can be difficult and, at times, uncomfortable, but leaders cannot let this slide. They must create, support, and ensure a culture of accountability for this leadership team and organization.

Finally, Lencioni suggests that the most effective teams focus on collective goals, not unit goals. Leaders can facilitate this by what they emphasize, measure, and celebrate. This process is facilitated if new members have this orientation to begin with, and are also oriented to this approach early in their tenure as a member of the team. Leaders can build this into the culture of their teams through their words and actions. Other members need to be encouraged and acknowledged for demonstrating this orientation through their words and actions. Soon this will become the norm for the highly functional team.

As noted above, a team approach to leadership has captured the imagination of contemporary leadership theorists. Leaders would be well-served in implementing this leadership style in their day-to-day practices, with members of their leadership team, and within the units that comprise their organization. Once assembled, members of the leadership team must actively and willingly share their perspectives with their leader and team members in meetings with the goal of ensuring that the best decisions are made, widely communicated, and effectively implemented. Productive conflict is not only desired – it is necessary to help ensure the best decisions are made.[100] Empower and inspire the leadership team by actively mining their opinions and channelling their intelligence, experience, and commitment. Encourage dissenting opinions as a strategy for fostering deeper thinking and consideration of more and perhaps better strategies. A leader and their leadership team should never differ on values but always be open to productive debate on strategies and decision-making. It can lead to better decisions, greater commitment and engagement, and heightened clarity of plans and aspirations. For example, consider the strategic direction of an organization. Effective leaders ensure that all key stakeholders have input and feel involved in determining a way forward. Colleagues will be more committed to the plan and its realization if they genuinely feel that their opinions are heard, even if they do not see their ideas in the final decision.

Engagement is critical at this stage of the process. Clarity and simplicity are critical and the next stage of the process. Leaders and members of their leadership teams need to take the ideas and perspectives forwarded and use their experience and insights to develop a clear and simple "vision and values" statement that they (and other unit leaders) can clearly, repeatedly, and convincingly articulate, along with an agreed- upon plan for making it a reality. Goals must be articulated, recorded, and progress evaluated in a clear, measurable, and time-bound fashion. Unit performance against these goals needs to be measured and celebrated. Leaders also need to ensure that they have the resources and support systems in place to attain and sustain positive change for their organization. Implementing things that have worked in the past, studying and adopting the "best practices" of comparable organizations, networking with other industry leaders, and asking insightful questions of other leaders about the types and levels of support they have in place will help leaders determine their support needs.

## LEADERSHIP PRACTICE #3 - EXERCISE GOOD JUDGEMENT

Leadership experts Warren Bennis and Noel Tichy once described "judgement" as "the essence of leadership."[101] I couldn't agree more. Leaders are called upon to make decisions on a number of areas ranging from human resources, strategy, and processes. Some decisions are relatively trivial and can be quickly made. Some are monumental decisions with dire consequences if wrong. A leader's judgement in these times is critical, and as Tichy and Bennis noted, it really is the *essence of leadership.*" As leaders progress in their careers and hopefully into elevated positions of influence, the importance of their decisions is magnified, as are the consequences of getting them wrong. Their decisions often have far-reaching implications and affect the lives of more people. Leadership and the judgement required to make the best decisions possible are not for the faint of heart.

> Reason and calm judgement are the qualities specially belonging to a leader.
>
> —TACITUS

Barack Obama poignantly highlights this reality in his insightful memoir entitled *A Promised Land.*[102] He chronicles many of the challenging decisions (e.g., to be a candidate, key appointments to his leadership team, crisis management, strategy, and international relations) that he was required to make as the 44th President of the United States. Some decisions needed to be immediate. Others required deeper thought and consultation. He wrote about getting the best information possible and the "smartest people in the room" to assist in making the best possible decision. He considered the "probability of outcomes" and encouraged his team leaders to do the same. Many decisions needed to be made based on inconclusive evidence. Other times he had to make decisions that were not ideal and far from perfect, but just better than the alternatives. A review of this book

## ADVANCING THE MANDATE

I met with the Provost shortly after I arrived at Western University and he highlighted something that I had previously read in the external review. He was a firm and direct leader, and he bluntly stated that The Faculty that I had just assumed leadership of "needed to be more research active". I knew it to be true and after discussing the issue with my leadership team, they agreed. We committed to tackling the issue head on.

Our first priority was benchmarking our performance in the area. We gathered data on our colleagues' books, research articles, research grants, research grant applications, and grants. While we had considerable work to do, we were more research active than campus leaders thought. We needed to change performance and perception.

We made advancing research a top priority. It was the centrepiece of addresses I delivered as well as those delivered by members of the leadership team to their stakeholders. I included member research achievements in my bi-weekly communication updates to members. We created new positions to support heightening research in the Faculty including a dedicated Grants Coordinator to assist with assembling competitive grant proposals, bring opportunities to the attention of our members, and assemble research teams to respond favourably to research grant calls. We added research technicians to support our researchers. We created internal grant competitions to get our members working more effectively together and help them establish a track record of success that would make them more competitive in national competitions. We created a Faculty Research Awards Committee to ensure that our members were competitively nominated for prestigious research awards. We staged Faculty-based Research Days to highlight the research activities of our members. We secured funds to establish Research Chairs, and we invested in Research Centres and thematic, pan-Faculty laboratories to support collaborative research projects and increase research activity. We continued to measure our progress, and we were pleased, but not totally satisfied with the results. Publication rates rose from 2.3 publications/per member per year to 3.6 per member/per year. The number of active grants in the Faculty went from 208/year to 340/year. Our success in the most prestigious

> grants jumped by 58% the first year, and 280% the second year where it stabilized. Research income significantly rose, as did the number of prestigious research prizes being awarded to our members. We continued to highlight the importance of research and we celebrated success along the way. Colleagues were clear about our priorities. A great leadership team ensured that they filtered down to our members.
>
> To hold us accountable, we then created an annual Research Report that summarized and charted our research activities and success and we published and widely distributed the document each year. It became a source of pride in the Faculty and helped embed the research culture that exists in the Faculty almost 20 years since that initial meeting with the Provost.

reinforces the importance of exercising good judgement that Tichy and Bennis outline in their insightful book.[103] The decisions leaders need to make as their careers progress become increasingly complex and usually impact more people, positively or negatively.

> History and the generations to come will judge our leaders by the decisions they make in the coming weeks.
> —NELSON MANDELA

Leaders must make decisions, and their impact and legacy is generally linked to the quality of their decisions. Leaders must do all they can to get the majority of their decisions correct. This is the most significant value that leaders bring to their group or organization. At times, leaders must make quick decisions based on inconclusive evidence. Other times leaders would be well served in employing the insightful processes and strategies outlined by behavioral economics researcher Daniel Kahneman so they do not rush to judgement but effectively gather as much information as possible and effectively mine the opinions of others who may have different perspectives and information.[104]

> Once you make a choice, you are saying 'yes' to the consequences of the decision.

In the end, leaders are accountable for the decisions they and the members of their senior leadership team make. Accountability rests with the leader. The best leaders surround themselves with strong, competent leaders who share the leader's values and have the courage and confidence to contribute to the decision-making process. If so, these leaders will speak up. They will appropriately challenge a leader's perspective as well as those of other members of the team. They will expect their ideas to be challenged as well. The best leaders bring this perspective to the decision-making table and reinforce the cultural norm that colleagues challenging a leader's perspective is not only welcomed but expected. These leaders also delegate trivial decisions and focus on the higher level people, strategy, and crisis management decisions that are critically important to a leader's long-term success. Once a decision is made, they take action and hold themselves and others accountable for the results. They know that they can always take corrective action if they have it wrong, but they do not remain in a state of "paralysis by analysis." After all, decisions without action, appropriate measurement, and accountability remain mere dreams.

> If you obsess over whether you are making the right decision, you are basically assuming that the universe will reward you for one thing and punish you for another.
> —DEEPAK CHOPRA

## LEADERSHIP PRACTICE #4 - ENSURE AN INSPIRING, FOCUSED, STRATEGIC, VALUES-BASED VISION

Nothing is more frustrating to colleagues in any endeavour than not knowing what they are doing, why they are doing it, or what is expected of them. Leaders must ensure clarity and clear direction. Note that the word "ensure" does not necessarily imply that the direction is always the leader's vision. In fact, in many cases, it isn't. Effective leaders build great leadership teams and establish a culture where colleagues are encouraged to share dreams, hopes, and aspirations. They find it inspiring. It also leads to great ideas being advanced, and the leader and the leadership team can then use their experience and insights to evaluate options and refine and communicate the selected option. Once determined, the leader, and the leadership team engages others so that colleagues are clear about what the unit is attempting to accomplish.

> We are kept from our goal not by obstacles but by a clear path to a lesser goal.

A basic tenet of leadership is the process of striving towards a shared aspiration. Leaders, and those they lead, need to know what the organization is attempting to accomplish. It is the "why" in Simon Sinek's exceptional book "*Start with Why: How great leaders inspire everyone to take action.*"[105] Colleagues need to know the plan, their role in bringing it to life, and the status of the plan. Effective leaders pay close attention to drawing attention to monitoring progress in these three areas. Developing and advancing an exciting and progressive vision that resonates with those charged with making it happen is an arduous process that takes the investment of time and energy. Some may wonder if the vision should be created before getting the team assembled. I concur with the guidance of Collins and Hansen[106], who suggested that leaders build a great team first and then engage these leaders in the creation of a great vision for the unit. Leaders and their leadership teams can then enact a process to identify, test, and validate the aspired values for their organization. Engaging colleagues and other stakeholders in this process is critical to help ensure acceptance, understanding, and commitment to bringing it to life.

An example of how this process can unfold can be taken from my last Decanal post at Western University. After assuming the role and taking the time to meet members and stakeholders and better understand the opportunities and issues, my leadership team and I embarked on a highly ambitious but important process to identify and clarify the Faculty's values, formulate our strategic vision, and prepare a number of objectives (with accompanying accountabilities and timelines for completion) that would help move the Faculty forward in a strategic and united fashion. We studied and integrated the strategic direction of the institution (i.e., heighten student engagement, advance interdisciplinary research and teaching programs, grow graduate programs, and create performance indicators in the teaching, research, and service areas).

The process took one year to complete, and it was time well spent. It helped crystallize the Faculty's direction and purpose. We deployed a high level of discipline to the process. It led to the development of a *Faculty of Health Sciences (FHS) Strategic Plan* that was values-driven and founded on extensive consultation, reflection, and discussion with numerous stakeholders (i.e., professors, staff members, students, alumni, and campus and community partners).

The process began with a census survey of the stakeholders (i.e., student leaders, staff, professors) to garner wide and full input on the values held by the Faculty, as well as gather members' perspectives on the strategic priorities that should be pursued. Each stakeholder was then invited to sit on one of five FHS Task Force Committees designed to help us (a) heighten and enrich the student experience and prepare graduates to be global leaders; (b) advance our research and scholarship; (c) increase our engagement with alumni, and the campus and communities;(d) expand our institutional and international partners; (e)increase our efficiency and diversify our resource base, and; (f) ensure that the FHS is a "great place to work, study, learn and grow".

The Task Force Committees met over the year, reviewing relevant data gathered from the survey, engaging in brainstorming and reflection sessions, hosting focus group sessions with members and stakeholders, and preparing a formal presentation that would be delivered to all members at the Faculty-wide retreat. Task Force Committee presentations at the retreat were followed by a series of small group and plenary discussion sessions designed to thoroughly test, validate or discard, and in some cases, extend the ideas forwarded by the working groups. All information collected was considered in the drafting of the Faculty Strategic Plan. Information that was important but not strategic was noted in an FHS Improvement Document, and these ideas were immediately pursued following the retreat. We also celebrated and incorporated the identified values, and they are captured in a concept we called CLEAR:

1. Community: The Faculty is made of diverse elements working together to achieve the vision of the Faculty within a caring community. A sense of community was sought where all members were engaged in the happenings of the Faculty, and they could come together socially and informally and through the *Dean's Update*. We will ensure Mutual Understanding, Mutual Meaning, and Mutual Respect within the Faculty.

2. Leadership: The FHS needed a clear, concise, and inspiring vision that aligned and activated current and future members. Colleagues sought input and wanted active and engaged leadership at all levels throughout the Faculty. They called on all colleagues to be positive, honest and supportive, effective communicators, honour achievement, and employ a team approach to leadership.

3. Expectations: Members expected to be treated fairly, to have a voice, and to have their contributions appreciated. In turn, the Faculty leaders could expect stakeholders to diligently perform to meet the expectations of their role.

4. Appreciation: Members sought to be appreciated for their accomplishments and, in turn, looked forward to working in a unit that valued commitment and contribution.

5. Respect: Mutual respect for individuals was identified as the foundation of a positive workplace culture. Members sought a workplace culture that eliminated harassment, increased respect between co-workers, and allowed all voices to be heard

and considered. Stakeholders also pledged to respect and welcome diversity of opinion.

The CLEAR concept, and the values that underlie it, governed behaviour across the FHS and served as the blueprint for decision-making for team members. These values were clearly and repeatedly articulated, communicated, and celebrated in formal and informal communications. They were widely shared across the campus, and their adherence at the School levels was an accountability measure for each School Director. The School Directors and their staff members were encouraged to take every opportunity to speak to external audiences about the Faculty, what it stands for, its strategic direction, and how it contributes to the overall mission of the institution.

The draft plan was shared with other campus Deans and campus leaders with a view of increasing inter-Faculty synergy. The draft document was also posted on the FHS web site and stakeholders were invited to provide feedback. The document was also shared with alumni and community partners, and their input was invited and considered prior to the plan being formally developed and approved at a special meeting of the Faculty Council. These steps allowed the FHS leaders to capture many ideas and perspectives and create a crisp, focused, and progressive strategic blueprint for the Faculty that served the unit extremely well.

Ensuring an inspiring, clear, and measurable strategic direction that is based on clearly articulated values is critical for a leader. The process of uncovering and articulating this blueprint must be a highly participative one. Leaders would be well served to employ a process like the one outlined above that engages the hearts, minds, and spirits of members in the creation of an inspiring strategic document that they own and are committed to bringing to life.

Average leaders raise the bar on themselves. Good
leaders raise the bar for others. Great leaders inspire
others to raise their own bar.

—ORWIN WOODWARD

## LEADERSHIP PRACTICE #5 - COMMUNICATE OPENLY AND HONESTLY AND FROM AN EMOTIONAL INTELLIGENCE BASE

Leaders must take opportunities to communicate clear and consistent messages effectively. They must make goals clear and public. They must also measure their progress towards their attainment and celebrate successes along the way. This is particularly important early in a leadership term when members are anticipating change and want to be assured that things will be different[107]. Effective and consistent communication is fundamental to strong leadership. Leaders must provide the right information to the right people, at the right time and of course, for the right reason. Providing this information in this format is one of the leader's most important responsibilities. Leaders must communicate frequently, consistently, and honestly. Great leaders ensure organizational clarity by "over-communicating" their message. They leave nothing to chance. They make goals clear and public. They focus their members by measuring organizational performance against clear, specific, and time-bound objectives. Stakeholders understand what both the organization and the leadership team value and how both will operate. The key rests in both the clarity and consistency of the message.

Engaging members goes well beyond keeping them informed. Leaders who share information freely and frequently also send the signal that they care about their members, that they value them, and they want them to be a part of a way forward. Contemporary leadership scholars[108] would coin this as an overt way of demonstrating emotional intelligence (EQ). An emotionally intelligent approach to leadership will appear to be counterintuitive to those who hold the opinion that leaders must be strong-willed, driven individuals who command and control their followers. Do not be fooled by this perspective. The latest developments in the area of leadership speak to the need for leaders to genuinely care about those in their charge (e.g., servant leadership) and to be focused on understanding and appealing to their emotions. An emotionally intelligent leader appears to let go of power, appears vulnerable at times, and focuses largely on the emotional needs of their members. However, this approach gets results.

Emotionally intelligent leaders ask and inspire members of the leadership teams rather than direct them. These leaders must be self-confident, committed to those they lead, and sensitive to their own emotional needs as well as those of their members. They work hard to build strong, trusting relationships with members of the leadership team. They awaken their curiosities, heighten their levels of commitment, and channel member energies to the accomplishment of organizational goals.

> Emotions are powerful drivers of their people's moods, and ultimately, performance.[109]

The exciting developments in the emotional intelligence area are especially applicable to contemporary leadership and current and prospective leaders would benefit from learning and applying the concept. Emotionally intelligent leaders engage and inspire followers by demonstrating their genuine interest in them. Followers know that their leader cares for them and trusts them with information. Followers feel respected and valued. The higher a person rises in an organizational hierarchy; the more important emotional intelligence is to their success[110]. An emotionally intelligent leader is self-aware, confident, demonstrates genuine care and concern for others, and manages their own emotions effectively. They actively listen to others. They have the willingness to slow down, step back, suspend judgement, and listen to the thoughts and perspectives of others who genuinely feel heard. They project a sense of calm and a feeling of confidence amongst those they encounter. Emotional intelligence is the key to effective leadership. Goleman's research points to an 85% correlation between emotional intelligence (EQ) and executive leadership success. He further states that EQ is greater than IQ when it comes to leadership effectiveness. Great leaders inspire the hearts and minds of others. Engagement is the solution. Effective communication is the means.

> The single biggest problem in communication is the illusion that it has taken place.
> —GEORGE BERNARD SHAW

Leaders need to effectively communicate at the macro and micro levels of the organization. They need to take the valuable opportunities afforded them at town hall and regular meetings to reinforce the vision and values of the organization, to acknowledge and trumpet the success of the unit and its members, and to highlight the upcoming challenges and opportunities that will help advance the organization. These formal platforms must be augmented with less formal communication programs. Leaders must work the halls of their building(s), taking the time to visit with members informally and build a strong relationship with them. These cannot be one-way exchanges. Leaders need to invite feedback and questions to truly engage members in their organization.

Leaders must attend professional and social events held in the departments to help enrich and extend these relationships. They need to reach out to their members on a regular basis with *Leader Updates* (e.g., electronic newsletters) that advise members of important events happening in the organization or in the sector, inform members of opportunities and deadlines, and congratulate colleagues on special achievements. Parts of the *Leader's Update* can also be re-formatted and electronically circulated to other relevant stakeholders (e.g., retirees) who will also appreciate the information and the chance to hear from the leader at more regular intervals. Colleagues might also derive benefit from a *Leader's Blog* that is updated regularly. Social media platforms available to contemporary leaders provide another option for them to frequently and honestly engage with their stakeholders.

Leaders and members of the leadership team need to find ways to connect with their colleagues and keep them "in the know ." In this author's experience this process often starts from the time members are shortlisted as candidates for positions in our organization. Prior to their site visit, they would be sent information about the organization, including our goals, our success stories, and our inspiring vision for the future. As leader, the author would insist on a 30-minute meeting with all shortlisted candidates for any leadership role where the organization's vision and values would be discussed along with performance and operational expectations. Members who join the organization were clear about what is important, how they fit in the unit, and how they would be evaluated. There were no surprises, and colleagues could decide if this organization was where they wanted to invest their efforts. In 99.9% of cases, this approach heightened the candidates' desire to join the organization. Once hired, these members are invited to a lunch where they once again hear about the organization's vision and values, as well as the support systems that are in place to help them succeed. Finally, new members are introduced to all members of the organization at an annual Fall Garden Party where the leader had another opportunity to speak about the organization's vision, values, and success indicators before welcoming the new members to the organization and formally introducing them to their new colleagues. These processes help members understand what the organization is attempting to accomplish in the workplace culture areas, help activate the CLEAR concept, and in doing so, leave nothing to interpretation as its relative importance. They also serve to strengthen the culture and built a heightened sense of team.

Effective leaders communicate regularly, especially with their leadership teams. Regular communication meetings are also held with the leader's office staff members so they can be apprised of this information in advance of reading it in the *Leader's Update*. Members are instructed to bring information and questions to these meetings, in order for information to flow freely within an institution.

> Encourage dissent. Leaders should have associates who have contrary views, who are devil's advocates, "variance sensors" who can tell them the difference between what is expected and what is really happening, between what they want to hear and what they need to hear. There are too many naked emperors running around today.
>
> — WARREN BENNIS

Leaders can set the stage for this type of openness through their words and actions. They must do the same with members of their leadership teams. Leaders should frequently ask their members the simple question: "How can I be a better leader?" This encourages leaders to thank their members for the feedback before working diligently to implement their valid suggestions.

Leaders must also ensure that members of the leadership team have all the information required to participate in fruitful discussions at the leadership table. If members are going to be true partners in leading the organization, they must have all the information needed to make decisions. Leaders must be fully transparent with this group and keep them informed of issues and challenges so they can help find workable solutions. Members should bring department-based issues to the table and ask other leaders to share their "best practices". Colleagues should feel comfortable bringing issues that they can't get resolved to these types of meetings so other leaders can offer suggestions or strategies that they have successfully used to address similar issues. Members should also be encouraged to speak openly about issues and concerns pertaining to the department and/or the organization. This culture helps foster a sense of team and brings more committed minds to the decision-making process. Only then will leaders realize the true benefits of a team approach to organizational leadership.

Some leaders are more effective communicators and leaders than others. Some connect with people. Others do not. The recent advances in emotional intelligence may hold the key for leaders seeking to heighten their effectiveness. This is especially true in the case of inspiring and empowering members of the leader's leadership team. Authentic leaders take a genuine interest in their members. They seek members' opinions. They get to know their members (and their families) beyond the workplace. In doing so, they build powerful relationships that are foundational to authentic leadership. Great leaders understand the role that emotions play in the leadership process.

The emotional intelligence literature base is garnering greater attention from contemporary leadership scholars. The concept has direct applicability to organizational leadership. Leaders seeking to improve their performance would be well-served in studying and integrating emotional intelligence into their leadership practices.

Leaders must be aware of their emotions and recognize the impact of their words and actions on others. They must be able to maintain their composure, and listen empathetically to the needs, wants, and desires of their leadership team members. They must be clear and honest in all of their interactions. This is hard work, but the benefits are worth the investment. Boyatzis suggested that the best leaders understand that emotions are the "backbone of leadership."[111] Effective leaders bring the very best in those around them to the benefit of the organization and the specific unit that they lead.

Accomplished artists, musicians, writers, and leaders share a passion for what they are doing and demonstrate unwavering commitment. Creativity and uninterrupted thought are critical to the process. They build their "bunker" and protect their most creative time. Musician Gordon Lightfoot would book himself into hotel rooms and write music through the night. He would journal creative lyrics or chords for songs while on extensive canoe trips. Maya

Angelo followed a disciplined writing routine that had her at her desk every day from 7:00 a.m. and wrote until 12:30 p.m. every day[112]. Stephen King followed a similar routine. He identified the morning hours as his creative and productive time, and he protected it for writing. British novelist Anthony Trollope started writing each day at 5:30 a.m., and he committed to 150 minutes of writing each day. He monitored his progress by committing to writing 250 words every 15 minutes and 2500 words each session. If he finished a novel before completing a session, he would simply start a new one.[113] Unwavering discipline and a laser focus were the keys to their success and creativity. My bunker was my office, and consistent with the advice of John Thompson, outlined earlier in the book, I used this time to reflect critically on our performance. This time was critical to my success. When writing this book and others, I made a commitment to write 1000 works each day. That was my benchmark during this creative stage. I didn't worry about grammar, spelling, or syntax – just the 1,000 words daily. I would fix mistakes and polish the document during an editing process that required a more focused, critical lens. These unique processes worked well for me.

Leaders must work hard, be disciplined, and focus on the most important things. "To Do Lists" can be effective in reminding leaders of things they shouldn't forget, but as Gary Keller and Jay Paspsan eloquently highlight in their insightful book[114] entitled *The One Thing: The Surprisingly Simple Truth behind Extraordinary Results*, effective people prioritize their "To Do List" and focus on the most important things. They replace their "To Do" list with a "Success List". A leader's "Success List" must be smaller and focused. In my case, I focused on the performance of my Faculty (student applications, student success, research activities and outcomes, evidence of internal and external leadership, my professional development needs and those of my direct reports, and workplace culture). I especially focused on these priorities during my regular reflection sessions that I fiercely protected in my calendar. Readers are encouraged to review the vignette entitled "Just How Important Were Those Tasks" presented later in this book for a hard lesson I learned about separating the urgent from the important.

> There is no elevator to the top, only the stairs.

## LEADERSHIP PRACTICE #6 - MODEL AND ENCOURAGE CONTINUAL LEADERSHIP LEARNING AND DEVELOPMENT

Leadership is not easy. It takes a considerable investment of time, energy and foresight. However, as noted earlier, the task becomes manageable when a leadership team is recruited, focused, empowered, and inspired to share in the leadership role. That said, the leadership role remains a challenging position. As noted earlier, leaders can have a short shelf life. Many leave the role frustrated and happy to have the experience behind them. This doesn't have to be the case.

> A man who views the world at 50 the same as he did
> at 20 has wasted 30 years.
>
> —MUHAMMAD ALI

Effective leaders know that they must attract a highly competent group of full and part-time staff colleagues and inspire and empower them to higher levels of achievement. Effectively leading colleagues and developing them into strong leaders in their own right are both critical components of a leader's role. Leadership can be learned and improved[115], and if leaders are to enjoy long-term success in the role, they must also stay current with developments in the field. They must renew themselves. Ongoing professional development and renewal are both critical for the long-term success of leaders and their organizations. Leaders must model the way through their own behaviours and encourage and support the developmental needs of leadership team members.

A life is not important except in the impact that it has on the lives of others.

—JACKIE ROBINSON

Leaders are encouraged to review the work of Stewart Friedman and his concept of total leadership.[116] He invites leaders to expand and integrate their influence beyond the workplace and into their homes, their communities, and themselves. Leadership is ubiquitous, and leaders need to see themselves this way. Friedman encourages leaders to apply and integrate leadership into all of their life roles and, in doing so, be more effective, increase their personal, professional, and organizational productivity, and lead/model more enriching lives. He calls on leaders to invest more of their time in reflection, thinking, and planning and less time concerned with the micro issues of their day-to-day work life. This may be viewed as common sense to readers, but based on this author's experience and observations, it is not common practice.

Productivity isn't about being a workhorse, keeping busy, and burning the midnight oil. It's more about priorities, planning, and fiercely protecting your time.

—MARGARITA TARTAKOVSKY

Last but not least, leaders need to invest in themselves and in their team members. They must take the time to reflect, recharge, and be on a path of continual growth so they can effectively lead and model the way for their members. Host two-item agenda meetings with team members to focus deeply on the big issues. Take one hour every two weeks to study performance metrics, reflect on the unit's progress, consider the performance of the leadership team, and determine performance development needs and areas for improvement. Attend conferences and workshops to stay current in your field and in the leadership area, and support members of the leadership team to do the same.

> Groups or organizations lead by leaders who stop learning are blue ribbon indicators of a group in trouble, or soon to be in trouble.

Leadership is critical to the success and vitality of organizations, and leaders can always improve. Leaders would be well-served in seeing themselves as "a developing leader, watch other leaders, practise, and remain open to good coaching."[117] I enthusiastically agree. In many settings, leaders have term limits, and for good reason. We operate in challenging times, and leadership takes total commitment and extensive energy. Leaders should adopt Ronald Reagan's mantra and leave the unit or organization in a timely manner and with the organization or unit in significantly better shape than it was when the leader entered the role. Leaders who engage and inspire a strong leadership team, listen attentively, and ensure ongoing growth and development, can extend their shelf life and impact and help ensure that they leave the unit in better shape.

The role of a leader is a complex one that usually does not come with a playbook. Leaders are often recruited into the role because they have distinguished themselves in their careers. However, these skills may not be helpful and could be counterproductive to success in a leadership role. Leaders can heighten their effectiveness by evaluating their leadership behaviours and considering implementing the six leadership practices. Some may see the need to hit the reset button on their leadership style. An honest self-assessment and feedback from superiors, peers and direct reports will be needed to determine if the leader is delivering on all six of these leadership practices. Leaders should regularly ask themselves and their teams the following ten questions to ensure that they are incorporating the six leadership practices that facilitate success (and survival) in the role:

1. Do we have a strong and formidable leadership team?
2. Am I empowering and inspiring members of the team to exceptional levels of achievement?

3. Have we ensured clarity and focus in the unit, as evidenced by a clear, strategic, and inspiring vision for the unit?

4. Is this vision understood and adopted by all members of the leadership team and my colleagues in the unit?

5. Have we developed specific, measurable, and time-bound objectives that will help everyone determine if we are making progress toward realizing our vision?

6. Do I communicate openly, honestly, thoroughly, and frequently with members of the leadership team, the administrative staff, and members of the unit?

7. Do members of the leadership team communicate openly, honestly, thoroughly, and frequently with each other?

8. Do I employ the tenets of emotional intelligence in my leadership and communication practices with members of my leadership team, the administrative staff, and colleagues in the unit?

9. Do we take the time to reflect on our leadership effectiveness and invest in commensurate leadership development activities when appropriate?

10. Do I invest in the leadership and professional development of colleagues on the leadership team members as well as the members of the administrative staff?

The need for strong and effective leadership has always been present, but recent times may be placing a higher premium on and calling for strong and effective leadership. Crises such as those brought on by the recent economic downturn require strong, passionate leadership that embodies the thinking of the top leadership minds whose concepts are profiled in this article.

> A smooth sea never produced a strong mariner.[118]
> —BILL GEORGE

There will be more choppy times ahead for leaders, and hopefully, the implementation of the six practices will facilitate their success. Effective leadership is a journey, not a destination. Leadership theorists consistently agree that the investment of time and energy invested in support of this leadership style will pay significant dividends for academic leaders, and by extension, for those they lead and serve. Leaders who deploy the six practices are well on their way to success and survival in the role.

> Success is no accident, it is from hard work, perseverance, learning, studying, sacrifice, and most of all, love of what you are doing.
>
> — PELE

## SUMMARY

What are the keys to success in leadership roles? Are there tried and true practices that best leaders consistently employ? I believe that there are, and leaders can always improve in these areas.

Leaders must get off to a great start. Print and electronic media sources are filled with examples of leaders who derail their impact by getting off to a poor start. I always made it a point to give new members of my leadership advice on how to navigate these early days when all eyes are on the leader. The ones who do this well intently listen. They seek to understand, not to be understood. They project hope and confidence, as well as show colleagues that they care about them and value their contributions. They work hard to better understand the culture of a group or organization. They reflect deeply on the performance of the unit and of people, especially members of their leadership team.

Effective leaders surround themselves with great leaders who bring complementary skill sets and perspectives to the table. They agree on values and know that strategy is always a debatable topic.

They engage and inspire these colleagues who pay their leader back with loyalty, appropriate challenge, and commitment. They also ensure that there is clarity of purpose. Nothing frustrates colleagues more than not knowing what they are doing, should be doing, or how their efforts contribute to the attainment of a pre-determined plan. Great leaders insist on this quality. Naturally, the vision is not always the idea of the leader, and in fact, many times it isn't. However, effective leaders ensure that there is clarity and focus throughout the unit or organization. The ideas often come from others, and leaders and their leadership team members can use their experience and insights to shape the ideas into a clear and compelling vision that is continually and effectively communicated and shared through the stakeholder communities.

> I have nothing in common with lazy people who blame others for their lack of success. Great things come from hard work and perseverance. No excuses – dedication sees dreams come true.
>
> —KOBE BRYANT

Communication is critical, and the best leaders actively and effectively communicate with colleagues. They involve and engage them in a way that people feel valued, supported and appreciated. Finally, leaders and their teams are always a work in progress. They must remain progressive and current. The best leaders strategically model and encourage continual learning. They invest in themselves and others to ensure that the group they are leading is on the frontiers of development in their respective fields.

GEAR

# THE REBIRTH/RENEWAL OR TIME TO EXIT PHASE

## A READER'S GUIDE:

Upon reading this section, readers will understand:

- the signs and signals that their impact and influence are wearing off;
- making the decision to stay and revitalize or leave the role;
- how to ensure a graceful and dignified exit;
- finding a mentor to assist with planning and executing the transition;
- the importance of succession planning;
- onboarding a successor, and then getting out of the way;
- balancing support for the successor and avoiding meddling in the business of the successor, and;
- the importance of having a "second mountain" to climb.

## CAN LEADERS STAY IN THEIR ROLES TOO LONG?

Bookshelves are filled with titles designed to help leaders excel in the role. My recent book, entitled *The 5C Leader: Exceptional Leadership Practices for Extraordinary Times* is an example of such a book. Leadership workshops and seminars typically focus on this stage in the leadership lifecycle. Far fewer authors have focused on helping people strategically prepare for leadership opportunities so I am pleased to help fill that gap in the early sections of this book. However, what follows is a relatively unique contribution to the leadership literature.

Some researchers have explored the topic in education. For example, Early and Weindling[119] studied school leaders' tenure and school performance and concluded that performance tended to diminish after a leader's eighth year in the role. They found that school leaders were generally most effective in their third to seventh year in the post, but many reached a plateau stage at year eight and school performance subsequently declined. Fidler and Anton's[120] study of school headmasters prompted them to arrive at a similar conclusion. They determined that the teachers' levels of job satisfaction and performance were negatively impacted by leaders who overstay their welcome. Ironically, many leaders investigated admitted that after 10 years in the role, they didn't have the same enthusiasm for the post as they had earlier in their tenure.

Similar findings emerged in studies[121] set in the food and computer industries. CEOs interviewed in this research admitted to growing stale in the leadership role and to not paying as close attention to the external environment. The CEO's admitted to not listening as openly or attentively, and they agreed that they were less open to new ideas and perspectives. Even the most effective senior leaders should reflect on these findings. Does it describe them? Would their direct reports agree that their leader rushes to judgement and doesn't listen as attentively as they would like? That said, it is clear that outside of these few studies, readers won't find much literature on this inevitable area of the leadership life cycle. This section of the book attempts to address this shortcoming.

In the following pages, readers will review a vastly unexplored area in the leadership literature, namely deciding how, and when, to leave a leadership role. This is a challenging stage for many leaders who stay in these roles too long, destroying their legacy and negatively impacting all of the gains their unit made in the early stages of the leader's tenure. Leaders can avoid that scenario. There is a science to this stage as well and I am delighted to cover this area and provide current and aspiring leaders with a blueprint to help them effectively and strategically navigate this critical stage in the leadership lifecycle. However, before we enter that section of the book, and I suggest that it is a critically important one, there are things that leaders can do to renew themselves and the efficacy of their influence over others. This will give the leader more time in the leadership role. However, be mindful of the fact that even the best leaders eventually leave leadership roles. After all, departure is inevitable at some point.

Yes, it should not come as a surprise to readers that all leaders eventually leave the leadership role. Some depart on their terms, others on the terms of committees or Boards. The late, great Bill Walsh, the former coach and General Manager of the San Francisco 49ers once poignantly suggested that a decade in any leadership role is long enough, and in some cases, it is too long. Henderson's research confirmed the same 10-year watermark.

> It is better to leave a leadership role two years early,
> than stay two months too long.

According to a 2018 PWC study[122] of the top 2,500 worldwide public companies suggested that early CEO departure was at a record high. According to their data, only 19% of CEOs stay in their leadership role for 10 years or longer. The researchers of that study also noted that the median tenure for CEOs was only five years. Leaders often stop learning, don't stay current, or lose their energy and edge. When this happens, it is long past the point when leaders need to change, or perhaps, they need to be changed. This book was designed to help leaders recognize the signs and symptoms that can inform their decision to renew or vacate the leadership role. As noted, it is often a painful, emotionally charged decision because far too many leaders identify themselves through the position or job title. Still, others know that they will miss the perks, prestige, and salary associated with the role and, consequently, are reluctant to give them up. Ironically, very few scholars have studied this inevitable area of the leadership lifecycle, but those who have done so[123] come to the same conclusion that a leader's impact often wanes, and many point to the 10-year mark as the outside limit for staying in the leadership role, even for the most effective leaders.

> Complacency is a leader's kryptonite. It impedes the emergence of brilliant ideas, stifles creativity and enthusiasm, and significantly inhibits a leader's efficacy and impact. Recognize it and conquer it before others do and conquer you. Change or be changed.

Stanley Bing is another example of the small number of authors who have written on the topic of a leader's "shelf life." His humorous book, entitled *The Big Bing: Black Holes of Time Management*[124] chronicles an executive's leadership shelf life across five inevitable stages and draws analogies to a food product going from being fresh and desired to perishable. Bing labels the five stages in the leadership lifecycle as: (a) fresh and neatly packaged; (b) mature and very tasty; (c) starting to turn; (d) ready for the platinum dumpster, and; (e) burial at sea. As noted in this book, leaders can extend their freshness through disciplined and conscious effort and can leave the leadership role on their terms and with grace and dignity. Unfortunately, many do not, and their tenure in the leadership role follows Bing's model.

According to Bing, the fresh and neatly packaged leader is early in their tenure. These leaders are typically keen and excited about the leadership opportunity and the progress of their units. At this stage, they are a sponge for learning and are always open to new ideas and possibilities. Followers are excited to be part of an exciting unit. They mature in the role. They build on small wins and springboard from them. They mature as a leader, remaining open to learning and listening. However, with time, things start to change. They find themselves stating that they tried this and that in the past, and it didn't work. Their instincts and experience often impede them from being open to new ideas and possibilities. They get a bit comfortable and start to rest on their laurels. They often burn out, become frustrated, and in some cases, bitter. They wonder how stakeholders could appear to be so disloyal and tuned out. They are seen as stale, disengaged, and ineffective. Followers begin counting down the days to when the leader will depart. Senior stakeholders begin devising strategies to remove the leader. The leader often doubles down on their authority to make decisions and prove that they are right. The organization suffers, as does the leader's impact and legacy. They quickly move through the stages of being ready for the platinum dumpster and being buried at sea.

The next section of the book will help leaders understand the signs and signals that their leadership impact is waning, and it is in their best interest, and the interests of the organization and relevant stakeholders, for them to leave the leadership role strategically and effectively.

## SHOULD I STAY OF SHOULD I GO?

The 1980s British Punk rock band "The Clash" posed the question in their famous song that leaders often face, namely, should I stay or should I go? All leaders eventually depart leadership roles – some by their own choosing and on their schedule, and some due to a decision that others make on their behalf. This book was prepared to help leaders make the right decision for themselves and their organization. Application of the contents will help leaders recognize the clues that will inform that decision. Those wishing to extend their leadership impact are provided with the strategies designed to help them renew. Those who choosing to leave are provided with guidance to help them do so you with grace, dignity, and the comfort of knowing that their successor has been prepared and onboarded to facilitate future success and prosperity. However, reading the signals and understanding the process takes a great deal of self-awareness and confidence. Leaders must be honest with themselves. According to Sills[125], with time, leaders run the risk of getting too comfortable in the leadership role. They rely too much on their instincts and past practice. They lose their edge, and the organization they are leading often gravitates into a downward spiral. Weak colleagues surrounding this leader often just get in line and don't push new ideas forward. Their development as future leaders becomes stunted.[126] All told, this is a bad situation, but one that is avoidable. Leaders need to be self-aware and understand the clues that it is time to revitalize or depart. Ideally, they should come to a decision themselves. They may need to move on if they can't legitimately revitalize themselves to meet ongoing and upcoming challenges. If they can't see it themselves, they need strong leaders around them who will give it to them straight. The best feedback is honest feedback, even if it means highlighting the reality that it is time for the leader to think about new challenges. Weak associates tell leaders what they think the leader wants to hear. Great, loyal associates tell them what they need to hear. They need to know the detrimental effect that they can have on their organization and their legacies if they are blind to the fact that they may be staying in the role too long and for the wrong reasons. Unfortunately, many leaders can't read, or they ignore the signals and, consequently, overstay their welcome. As a result, their organizations and their leadership reputations significantly suffer.

> Only those who risk going too far can possibly find out how far one can go.
>
> —T.S. ELIOT

# LEADER SELF-AWARENESS

According to Goleman and his colleagues[127] the best leaders have heightened levels of emotional intelligence, and self-awareness is the foundation of the concept. Contemporary leadership scholars have noted that the best leaders have an acute sense of their strengths and weaknesses as well as the efficacy of their impact.[128] High-performing leaders have a higher level of self-awareness, and they know when they are reaching the end. They understand the need for revitalization or departure before others do.

Self-awareness should be a major skill that is considered when identifying potential leaders, developing potential leaders, and selecting potential leaders. Self-awareness is a critical part of emotional intelligence, which has been identified as the key ingredient to success in leadership.[129] It is important to note that a heightened level of self-awareness can serve leaders beyond succeeding in the role. It can also be invaluable in helping leaders gauge their efficacy and help them determine if it is time to revitalize or move on to other things. These leaders know when they are performing well, are excited about new processes, are sensitive to the leadership development needs of colleagues on their leadership teams and are open to new ideas and possibilities. More importantly, they also know when they have moved the unit as far as they can, when they are tired and less inspired, when they are not open to new ideas, and when they know that a new leader and new voice are required. They also understand that their legacy and reputation may be dictated by the decisions they make. History books are filled with examples of once-effective leaders staying on too long and tarnishing their impact and reputations.

> It ain't what you don't know that gets you in trouble. It's what you know for sure that just ain't so.
>
> —MARK TWAIN

Knowing when to step away from a leadership position calls on a leader's self-awareness and confidence. Leaders have generally spent time building their skill set and acquiring relevant experiences needed to emerge and excel as a great leader. They generally have an adept aptitude for recognizing their personal well-being and emotions. This skill, however, can diminish with time. Leaders in their roles for a long time might overlook the alarming cues that signal an expiring shelf life. They might stop. They may not pay as close attention to the threats and opportunities in their industry. They might begin to rely too much on their instincts and not enough on emerging trends or data. Researchers like Percy and Rossiter[130] studied this area and suggested that leaders should consider their impact and legacy of their brand. What reputation is important to them? Do they want to go down in history as a great leader who got things done and always had the best interest of the organization in mind, or a leader who didn't know when to quit and whose self-interests in holding on to the power and authority of the position was more important than the success of the organization? A leader's reputation is their brand. It is unique to the individual, the environment, and the position. Leaders need to ask themselves why they wish to stay in the position. Is it to serve and help others? Is it to move the organization forward, or might the true motives be personal ambitions (e.g., power, prestige, financial, emotional)? These are difficult questions to pose, but strong, confident, self-aware leaders are willing to take these questions on and answer them with integrity.

Jacobus[131] and Pienaar[132] are two researchers who arrived at the same conclusions in their research on ineffective leaders. These researchers concurred that leaders who have stayed too long in the role often become cautious and less open to new ideas or to taking calculated risks. They often become overly rigid and set in their ways. These approaches naturally stifle creativity, and soon colleagues stop offering ideas that could move the organization forward. They know their leader is not open to change.

Some will view the leader as arrogant. They may come across as a "know it all" person. They further suggested that narcissism often plays an underreported role in explaining why these leaders are so reluctant to give up their leadership roles. For some, their personal identity and self-worth are defined by their being in the leadership role,

## KNOWING WHEN IT IS TIME TO GO

I started my higher education journey in the Faculty of Human Kinetics at the University of Windsor. I loved the program, was mentored by a host of gifted professors, met some life-long friends, and played on the varsity hockey team. I loved the undergraduate experience so much that I decided to enrol in the graduate program where I worked closely with a number of professors and decided that a career in higher education was exactly the path that I wanted to pursue. I thought that I worked well with others and I believed, even then, that a decanal post would be my dream job. Little did I know that 15 years later, following a short academic post at another university and a PhD from The Ohio State University, and establishing a track record in a number of smaller administrative posts (i.e., getting my ticket punched), I would be entering the Dean's Office.

I loved the Dean's position, and especially loved the opportunity to work in this leadership role at my beloved alma mater. Collectively we enjoyed a great deal of success. Leadership teams were built, new hires joined a solid core, new programs were launched. We were riding a high. I was pleased when my colleagues renewed me for another five-year term. We had lots to do together. New facilities were added, enrolments soared, we were attracting and retaining the best and brightest students, professors, and staff members. However, about halfway through my second term I could see the light at the end of the tunnel. I held a personal belief that leaders can't over-extend their welcome and I was starting to feel the need for a change. Fortunately, a larger institution, The University of Western Ontario (now Western University) had just amalgamated three Faculties into a super Faculty and officials there were looking for an experienced leader who could bring that group together and advance it to new heights. While it was difficult to leave a role and an institution that held my affection so deeply, I knew that it was time to move on. We had accomplished a great deal during my time in office and it was time for some new ideas and energy. One of my Windsor Department Heads was well prepared to assume the Decanal post and I could leave the role at that time with the confidence and comfort of knowing that the place was in good shape and destined for sustained success. I also needed some new challenges – and with the support of my wife and children, we headed to London, Ontario and I joined Western University (known as The University of Western Ontario at the time) as the Dean of the Faculty of Health Sciences.

The Faculty of Health Sciences was ten times the size of my former Faculty. The unit was culturally fractured and needed change. Colleagues felt betrayed by the institution due to a recent restructuring and amalgamation. We needed to build trust, lift spirits, project calm, and inspire hope. I spent my early days visiting with colleagues and focused on building relationships. I listened to their issues and tried to keep things positive. I sensed that colleagues were ready to embark on a new day, and they were.

Campus leaders got behind the Faculty. We made some new hires to bolster a formidable core. Professional and social events were scheduled to bring colleagues together. Unit leaders formed a leadership team and they were advised that in addition to leading their units (and I would do my best to get them the resources needed), they were required to join me and help lead the Faculty. This was a key step in bringing the unit together. Colleagues thrived in this environment and colleagues on the leadership team thrived on the leadership team and sought term renewals.

The Faculty was performing well. New programs were launched and we were attracting the best and brightest students, including those winning major academic awards (and one who earned a Rhodes Scholarship). Our research metrics were also exploding. Programs were introduced to incent research activities and colleagues were winning some of the highest research awards offered in the academy. We built new buildings and helped position and prepare the Faculty for sustained success. Our faculty, staff and students were demonstrating incredible leadership on our campus, in the community, and in the profession. Best of all, and in harmony with our top priority, our Faculty was leading the institution in member engagement. Our efforts to change the culture were working and we were becoming a "great place to work, study, learn, and grow".

> I was pleased to be renewed for a second five-year term where we strategically worked to advance the Faculty. However, I knew that I would need a change, and the Faculty would need a change in leadership following that second term. Strategies were employed to get the next generation of leaders ready to compete for the role. Given the experience that members of my senior team had gained due to their longevity in the role and the degree to which they were empowered to lead, I was not surprised, but in fact delighted, when three of the four final candidates for the position came off of my leadership teams. Colleagues were ready, and decision makers considered them ready for the role. One was selected and she took office following the conclusion of my second term and the transition process was seamless. Following some onboarding activities, I enjoyed an administrative leave, then returned to campus in some new administrative capacities that took me away from the Faculty and "out of the hair" of the new leader. My new responsibilities offered a new set of challenges. The system worked for me and the Faculty. I left with colleagues wanting more, with a Faculty platformed for sustained success, and me with a chance to do other things. I was always available to the new leader, but consciously kept my distance to give the new leader the space needed to effectively lead.

and they are fearful of being minimized once outside the role. These researchers believe that self-interest, greed, and an unquenchable thirst for power are often the driving motives for leaders wishing to hold on to their leadership positions.

Unfortunately, research shows that many leaders overstay their welcome. A leader's extended stay could be the result of not wanting to step away (i.e., due to ego, prestige, power or uncertainty of their next step) or perhaps from not knowing how, or when to effectively step away. Those seeking guidance in this area will not find much help in the leadership literature. Leadership scholars have been very helpful in providing advice on how to prepare for leadership, and especially helpful in assisting leaders to excel in the role once assumed. Very little has been done on the inevitable departure. Leaders often need help in determining when, and how, to effectively depart a leadership role.

Finding a good mentor who has gone through the departure process can be invaluable. Learn from their experience. Ask them about how they navigated the process and determine if their practices might also work for you. They will be able to empathize with the departing leader and they will have the lived experience that can help the outgoing leader effectively depart, and do so with grace, dignity, and their legacy intact. Park your ego and ask questions that will help you deal with the loss of authority, power, prestige, and access to information. Ensure that you have something to look forward to, even if it is a short break before tackling new challenges and/or interests.

## A MENTORING DISCUSSION: LEAVING THE LEADERSHIP ROLE

I recently spent time with a retired colleague who held a major leadership role at my university. We talked about our times together around the leadership table and I commented on her effectiveness in the leadership role, and how she has managed her retirement. I asked her for her advice as I consider this stage in my career.

*"Yes,"* she said. *"I miss many parts of the leadership role. I liked the fact that I had responsibility for something big. I enjoyed having the authority to make decisions, and the resources to help younger colleagues develop their leadership skills. I also realized that I had become dependent on staff members for things. I realized that I didn't have someone to troubleshoot my computer issues, program my answering machine, or prepare my expense claims. I had to pay for my own cell phone and travel."*

She realized that she loved being on the point of key decisions. However, she said, *"I have also come to the realization that there is life after leadership. I love the chance to do things that I never had time to do in the past. There was a time when everything I read had a staple in the top corner. Now I read great literature. I attend theatre productions regularly. I go to concerts with my husband and friends. I meet people for casual lunches. Life is great. However, there is an adjustment period."*

She looked at me and said, *"here is what I recommend."*

Do not make any long-term commitments in your first year of retirement. Take the time to relax, recharge, and think about what you would really like to do. She took a year and focussed on her needs and interests.

She noted that she got calls from colleagues longing for the *"good old days."* Thank them for the call, but quickly remind them that they need to work with the current leader, and that they would honour you by giving the new leader the same level of loyalty and support that they gave you. A positive word about the new leader is very helpful at this stage of the conversation.

Following this year, and lots of reflection, get involved in organizations and causes you believe in. In her case, she joined two Boards. Each one meets quarterly so the commitment is not too onerous. She suggested that retiring leaders give more time to the hobbies they enjoy and challenge themselves by developing new interests. She enrolled in a continuing education program at her local university to pursue an interest in Canadian history. Finally, she suggested that departing leaders do the things that they really want to do. She noted that she and her husband liked to travel and they have made a list of places that they would like to see. She laughed and stated that *"it is a long list, but we are working our way through it."*

The only thing that I would add to my great colleague's list is the need to reflect on your emotions at every step of the way, and to be sure to throw the ladder down to departing leaders you encounter in the future and offer to help them work through the process. We need mentoring at the time of departure as much as we do upon entry.

Thanks Carol.

## INDICATORS AND WARNING SIGNS

Some people in leadership roles hang their identity on the position. Some worry about what they might do after they leave the leadership role. Still others love the power, the perks, the prestige, and in some cases, the financial rewards associated with leadership roles. They haven't grasped the reality that all leadership roles are temporary. Know that we all exit leadership roles eventually. My goal is to help leaders do it effectively, and with grace and dignity.

What are the cues and indicators that a leader has reached their peak and should be thinking about strategies to significantly renew their leadership practices (energy, ideas, perspectives) or be thinking that it is the right time to depart and find another mountain to climb? The three red flags that indicate leaders need to revitalize or depart are: a waning passion; being closed to new ideas and possibilities, and; feeling that the predetermined mission is now accomplished and the time is right for a new leader to come in who will bring new ideas, a new voice, and a different leadership style to the situation. Each of these indicators are discussed in the following section.

## INDICATOR #1: WANING PASSION

Leadership is hard work. Leaders are called upon to make difficult decisions. Leaders are always on and hold themselves accountable for the actions of those in their care. The role can be draining physically, emotionally, and mentally. Leaders must take the time to recharge and renew their energy stores, or they will ultimately burn out. Those who do not renew and recharge will undoubtedly soon lose their drive, or as leadership expert Noel Tichy called it, the "leader's edge."[133] Leadership responsibilities can wear a person down. It is completely natural. Some have higher threshold levels. Others have strong teams, and they maintain their energy levels and edge by effectively delegating. In addition, they renew and recharge their energy levels through sabbatical leaves and extended vacations. One way or another, leaders must stay upbeat, positive, and future-oriented. They must stay committed to ongoing learning and to seizing new opportunities when due diligence informs the decision to act. When leaders lose their edge and their passion for learning, they often rest on their laurels and are comfortable with the status quo. This is not conducive to sustained leadership effectiveness.

The best leaders have a high degree of emotional intelligence and are, therefore, self-aware. They have the capacity to read situations and assess their impact. They can tell if their passion for people, their industry, and for the rigours of leadership are waning, and if they are, they have the self-confidence and instincts to know that it is time to move on. They are also surrounded by other strong leaders who have the courage and confidence to bring this to their leader's attention. Their relationship is strong and respectful. Excellent team members display the courage and confidence to share the brutal facts with leaders. However, the best leaders, those with high degrees of confidence and self-awareness, know when it is time to move long before others see it. Unfortunately, many leaders lack this type of insight, stay in the role too long, and in doing so, often damage their organization or unit and deflate their reputation and legacy that they worked so hard to build. It doesn't have to be that way. The best leaders pay attention to the signals that indicate when they are losing their passion for the leadership role.

## TANK IS EMPTY – TIME TO DEPART

In late January, 2023, Jacinda Ardern surprisingly announced that she was stepping down as the Prime Minister of New Zealand. She was seen as a trailblazing leader who was revered across the globe for her exceptional leadership. Her strong leadership during the pandemic and again following the Christchurch terrorist attack were especially noteworthy. She was first elected to the position in 2017 and earned a ringing re-election endorsement in 2020. Why did she announce that she was leaving? She was crystal clear in her media conference – she had the self-awareness and confidence to admit that she was running out of gas.

As noted in the January 19, 2023 *CNN Report,* (*New Zealand leader Jacinda Ardern announces shock resignation before upcoming election*), Arden stated that "the decision was my own." She further noted that "leading a country is the most privileged job anyone could ever have, but also the most challenging. You cannot, and should not, do the job unless you have a full tank, plus a bit in reserve for those unplanned and unexpected challenges. I no longer have enough in the tank to do the job justice."

## INDICATOR #2: TENDENCY TO RUSH TO JUDGEMENT

Another indicator that it may be time to move on is when leaders catch themselves frequently falling prey to System 1 decision-making style (i.e., snap judgements based on past experience and instincts) when a slower, more deliberate decision-making process (i.e., System 2 decision-making style) is warranted. [134] Effective leaders are always learning and open to new ideas, opportunities, and perspectives when they are warranted.

Writers like Daniel Kahneman tangentially touch on the topic. In his classic book entitled, *Thinking, Fast and Slow*, Kahneman cautions leaders about the trials and tribulations of slipping into this pattern. Leaders need to have a high degree of self-awareness to recognize this troubling pattern and take corrective action once identified. Loyal associates can help them identify this fault. These signals can serve as an "alert" to an individual that they need to be more open, more inclusive, and if they don't change, their influence and leadership impact will be significantly derailed.

Judith Sills is one of the few leadership writers who has focused on the end of the leadership life cycle.[135] In her book, Sills presents a model that can be adapted to help explain the final stages of the leadership life cycle. Naturally, a precursor to employing this model is ensuring that leaders are not in denial or overestimating their impact. They must be brutally honest with themselves in assessing their leading impact and their energy and desire to keep learning and leading. Leaders can get comfortable in their role, and this comfort can often lead to negative impacts. Leaders must determine if they have the energy and desire to tackle new challenges, set new directions, embrace uncertainty, and work tirelessly in the role to help move the unit forward. Leadership is tough.

Sills outlined a seven-step action plan to help leaders who decide to stay in the role and believe they have the energy and desire to persevere and effectively lead their organization. These steps are: (a) face what hurts; (b) create a vision; (c) make a decision; (d) identify a pattern; (e) let go; (f) face your fear, and; (g) take action. Leaders must face the "brutal facts". [136] Am I effective? Am I listening as acutely as I did in the early years of my time as a leader? Am I open to exciting new ideas that align with our mission and values? Would the organization be better served with another leader or am I the right person at this time to lead the unit? Addressing these questions can be uncomfortable for leaders, but it is a necessary process for leaders to undertake to effectively lead their unit or organization over the long term.

In the final analysis, stakeholders need clarity about what the unit is doing, and why. They must have confidence that the vision for the unit makes sense. Leaders must ensure that a clear path forward is created and effectively communicated to stakeholders. The vision does not necessarily need to be created by the leader, and often times it isn't solely the leader's idea. However, the leader must insist on clarity of purpose and be sure that key participants are aware of the plan and invested in making it come to life.

Leaders must assess the culture of their unit. The best leaders ensure that a culture is in place that inspires the sharing of ideas, and leaders and/or their leadership teams can then use their experience to distill the ideas into a clear and coherent strategic vision for the group. [137] They may have to let go of their ideas and perspectives when they are convinced of better options or alternatives. They must be brave, confident and clairvoyant, and when action is required, they boldly enact it. As well, these leaders have colleagues around them who give it to them straight and tell them when they are "running with scissors."

> It is not the critic who counts; not the man who points out how the strong man stumbles, or where the doer of deeds could have done them better. The credit belongs to the man who is actually in the arena, whose face is marred by dust and sweat and blood; who strives valiantly; who errs, who comes short again and again,

because there is no effort without error and shortcoming; but who does actually strive to do the deeds; who knows great enthusiasms, the great devotions; who spends himself in a worthy cause; who at the best knows in the end the triumph of high achievement, and who at the worst, if he fails, at least fails while daring greatly, so that his place shall never be with those cold and timid souls who neither know victory nor defeat.

—THEODORE ROOSEVELT

## INDICATOR #3: FEELING OF MISSION ACCOMPLISHED

Effective leaders and organizations have a plan. They ensure that the unit they are leading has a clear focus and a metrics system to know when they have achieved what they set out to do. They have a clear finish line. They know when the goal has been reached. At this time, leaders often have a decision to make. Leaders have to decide if they have the energy levels and skill sets needed to further advance the unit. Sometimes they do. Other times they don't. Leaders need to have the self-awareness and confidence to know when it is time to move on. There are "horses for courses," and leadership styles and perspectives work better in some situations than others. The unit might require new energy, fresh perspectives, or a new voice.

This scenario is often played out in sports. A young, developing sports team usually needs a coach who is a teacher and nurturer. They need a leader who can develop their skills and provide them with the confidence needed to excel in the future. As their talent and confidence levels grow, they need a different type of leadership from the coach. They need a coach with an advanced skill set in strategy and motivation. The self-aware coach knows this, and if they are smart, step aside and find another coaching position better suited to their skill set. Those who don't often stick around and usually end up getting fired, which is disruptive to the team and to the coach's career. Those who navigate this reality well are self-aware and confident in their skills. The same scenario can play out in organizational life. Leaders need to remain focussed on their mandate and, once attained, realize that the mission is accomplished and it is time for a change.

Leaders must come to grips with the fact that everyone departs the leadership role eventually. Some are oblivious to the indicators and are often forced out, leaving them embarrassed and often bitter. Others effectively read the signals that it is time to change or depart. A leader's shelf life can be extended, and readers will understand how in the following sections. However, leadership is hard work, and it can be emotionally draining. It is why some suggest that leaders should not be in any role for longer than seven years.[138]

Leaders must be honest with themselves and the impact that they are having on their unit or organization and make the right decision for them and their unit or organization. They need to ask themselves questions like: Do I want to stay in the role? Do I have the interest and energy to perform admirably? In addition to being the leader, do I want to do the heavy lifting required of leaders? Do the majority of colleagues want me to stay in the role? Can I commit to the sacrifices required and to meeting the challenges that lie ahead? Do I have the energy, motivation and interest to serve in the role? In addition, does the unit or organization need a change? Honest answers to these questions will help the leader determine whether staying in the role and renewing their skills and talents or departing the role and engaging in some form of succession planning is best. Leaders must ask themselves tough questions and provide honest answers to these questions.

If serving is below you, leadership is beyond you.

Knowing when to step away from a leadership role requires a keen sense of self-awareness and a level of confidence that will support the decision. Some do this well, leave on their terms and do it with grace and dignity. Some decide to stay on but have the self-awareness and insight to know that they need to continue to grow as a leader, stay progressive in their industry, and be open to the ideas and development of other leaders in the unit. Still others stubbornly stay on when they shouldn't, bringing their unit or organization down in the process and destroying the leadership legacy that they may have taken years to build. They may not have the energy, enthusiasm, and vision needed to move the unit forward. They may be stifling the unit as well as the emerging leaders who seek opportunities for higher levels of engagement. The best leaders have high levels of emotional intelligence, and especially self-awareness, and they make the right decision at the right time. They leave the unit or organization at its peak, knowing that they have left the unit or organization in better shape than they found it and are ready to move forward under the leadership of the leader's successor. Those in the latter group may choose to hold on to the role for a variety of selfish reasons or not see or disregard the cues that signal that it is time to move on.

Leaders must understand the concept of a leader's shelf life. Can they continue to be progressive and effective? Are they willing to learn and reenergize so they can effectively keep their organization moving forward? Does the group need a new leader? Does the leader need new challenges? Being honest, being self-aware, knowing the signals that it is time to move on, having something else to look forward to, and getting some guidance from mentors who have gone through the process are all helpful pieces of advice.

> Leaving a leadership role can be painful and challenging, especially for leaders wishing to hold on to the role for selfish reasons. It is always best to leave a leadership role on your terms, with pride and dignity, and with a new role or phase in life to look forward to.

# DECISION TO STAY AND REVITALIZE

Leaders wishing to extend their role will be comforted by the knowledge that there are things that they can do to recharge their batteries and renew their influence. They don't have to leave. They can strategically re-energize and re-engage. Ulrich and Smallwood[139] offer insights and suggestions that can help a leader find their second wind and effectively stay longer in the leadership role. For example, they encourage leaders to spend time with other leaders who have been successful over a longer period of time and ask them to share their longevity secrets. Seek out leaders inside and outside your industry who have remained current and continually reinvent themselves. Try to emulate their practices. Better yet, ask them to mentor you on the keys to ensuring long-term sustainability in the leadership role. They will undoubtedly hear that they need to stay current in their field and in the leadership area. They may be encouraged to read biographies of great leaders and attend industry conferences and workshops focused on leadership. They will be told to read trade publications to stay current on the developments in their industry. Complacency is often cited as the number one reason why a leader's effectiveness begins to dissipate. They have been in the position a long time and believe they have seen everything. They are not open to new ideas and perspectives. Those who break the mould and extend their shelf life do so because they reinvent themselves. They break away from the complacency trap that inhibits many senior leaders. They understand that their fields get disrupted and maintaining a status quo approach often means that the organization and a leader's efficacy is in decline. Others simply burn out because they haven't taken the time to invest in themselves, their health, their growth, or in any outside interests.

Take a sabbatical if it is possible to recharge your batteries and develop some new skills and passions. If a sabbatical is not possible, perhaps a secondment into another temporary role would prove helpful in developing new skills and restoring the leader's energy levels. Sometimes a change is as good as a rest. Whatever the process, find a way to stay current, curious and hungry for information and continual growth. Leaders can extend their shelf life and extend their effectiveness by engaging in these practices.[140]

Lipner[141] suggested that practicing leaders can extend their shelf life by having other interests and, most of all, looking after themselves. They need to be active. Commit to a wellness program that puts their health first. Go for walks. Leaders should pursue outside interests and hobbies that they enjoy. They should meet and engage with more people outside the workplace. They should take time to invest in themselves and develop outside interests that take away from the burdens of leadership and make them whole. Leaders who make these types of investments in themselves don't burn out as quickly and, as a result, can extend their time and effectiveness in a leadership role. As well, it will put them in a good position when they do transition into retirement.

Leaders who feel that their impact may be diminishing will be comforted by the work of Boyatzis and his colleagues[142], who provide helpful guidance to leaders who feel like their impact may be waning, but they are not ready and willing to give up the leadership role. These authors believe that leaders can renew themselves and regain the leadership prowess that colleagues saw in them when they were initially appointed. Perhaps they need to participate in a small sabbatical or an extended vacation/leader development program to recharge their batteries and reflect on new leadership practices that will make them more effective. An additional benefit of this approach is that it creates an advanced leadership development opportunity for one of the members of the leadership team who fills in for the leader during their absence.

According to Boyatzis and his colleagues, leaders can extend their effectiveness and by extension, extend their shelf life by developing their emotional intelligence skills (i.e., their levels of self-awareness, their self-regulation habits, and heightening their empathy for others). They can also extend their impact by having a genuine hunger to learn and develop strong skills in active listening. Boyatzis and colleagues further suggested that leaders can also extend their effectiveness and their time in the role by increasing leader development opportunities for their direct reports, heightening their awareness and attention to social injustices, and finally, celebrating small wins and using them to build support for greater challenges.

Ulrich and Smallwood[143] offer support for leaders facing the end of their lifecycle through their START ME principle. They offer seven suggestions that leaders at this stage should consider to extend their shelf life and, consequently, maintain their impact in the leadership role. The seven principles are: (a) simplicity; (b) time; (c) accountability; (d) resources; (e) tracking; (f) melioration (i.e., resiliency), and; (g) emotion. Each of these principles is discussed in the following section.

Experienced leaders wishing to extend their shelf life will know that almost everything in organizational life is urgent, but far fewer things are important. Inboxes are rarely empty, and there is always something to do. Effective leaders know the difference between things that are urgent and things that are important, and they focus on getting the important things done first. These leaders have the ability and discipline to cut through the messiness of situations and try to simplify situations where possible. Don't let your instincts take over and therefore rush to judgement. Be aware that these tendencies happen. Take the time to reflect on the most important things and, where possible, apply your experience and insights to simplify them and communicate the analysis to stakeholders.

> Be like a postage stamp – stick to one thing until you get there.
>
> —JOSH BILLINGS

Long-term leaders know that their time is their most precious asset. Followers look to their leaders for an example of how to best spend their time. The best leaders effectively delegate important tasks and focus on the bigger, more strategic pieces. They regularly take time in their workweek to reflect on their unit's progress and the performance of their direct reports. They know that everyone needs to continually develop if the organization is going to succeed long term. They also invest time in

## JUST HOW IMPORTANT WERE THOSE TASKS

I became a Dean at a young age. While higher education institutions are getting better at preparing academics for leadership roles, this was not really the case in my early days. I was young and inexperienced. However, I was committed to hard work and putting in long hours. My wife and young kids went to bed early and I was a night owl. It was a time for me to catch up and get things done.

I would put so many things in my briefcase to take home at the end of the day that I eventually sprung the hinges on my briefcase. A larger briefcase proved some relief to my problem, but eventually my homework projects exceeded the capacity of the larger case. Instead of setting clearer priorities and focusing on them, I thought that I just needed a bigger carrying case. I found one on the floor of my office. The recycle bin was perfect. It didn't have a lid so I could pile projects high at the close of each workday. I clearly needed a lesson in separating the urgent from the important. I got that lesson – the hard way.

One night I was loading up my recycle bin when my office phone rang and my wife reminded me of the school concert we were scheduled to attend with the kids. It had slipped my mind, and I needed to leave the office immediately. I left my packed recycle box on my desk, filled to the brim with requests for meetings, seemingly important tasks to complete, and I headed for home and then to the concert.

The next morning, I arrived to find an empty recycle box. During the night, the cleaning staff had "recycled" the entire contents of my overflowed recycle box (i.e., my modified briefcase). Panic immediately set in, as I am sure it is setting in with readers. However, the irony was that not one person called later that day or week asking me why I missed a meeting or in search of a report I was supposed to draft. In fact, not one person ever called me to follow up on a missed assignment. It highlighted a couple of things for me. First of all, clearly not everything occupying my time at that point in my career was important. Secondly, this proved to be an incredible time management tool. From that day forward, I learned to set clearer priorities. I delegated more effectively. I said no to things that were not essential to my "Success List." I became a better leader by focussing my time and energy on the conceptual elements of my leadership role, and less on the details that previously robbed me of my time and energy.

leading others. They critically assess their performance and professional development needs and they invest in these colleagues. They also assess their own professional development needs so they can stay current in their field and in the area of leadership. They tend to spend considerable amounts of time reflecting, assessing, and strategizing. Ineffective leaders are constantly "chasing their tails." They are busy but often not focussed on the right things. Colleagues see this and begin to question their leader's impact and efficacy, leading to a shortened life cycle. Be aware of how you are spending your time on the things effective leaders need to focus upon.

> Even if you are on the right track, you will get run over
> if you just sit there.
>
> —WILL ROGERS

Leaders can enjoy long-term success. These leaders effectively marry a laser-like focus to an agreed-upon vision or strategy and ensure that they and others are held accountable to commitments designed to bring the vision to life. They follow through on commitments. If there is a chance they can't make a commitment, they say so at the start. They demonstrate a personal commitment and hold others accountable for their commitments. It is a key component to long-term success and survival in the leadership role. Effective leaders know it and ensure that accountability is a hallmark of their leadership practice.

We all need professional development. Organizations typically ensure professional development at the start of one's leadership career, but experts in the area[144] justifiably question why professional development needs to stop. Ideally, leaders at all stages of the leadership lifecycle need it. Professional development is especially important in the later stages of the leadership lifecycle to facilitate leaders remaining progressive and on the cutting edge of development in their industry and in the area of leadership. It helps keep them current, effective, and, truth be told, better suited to stay in the leadership role for longer periods of time. Professional development can take many forms, from professional conferences, workshops, and in-house or off-site leader development programs. Leaders wishing to extend their time in a leadership role would be well served in securing a mentor (within the industry or outside the industry) who is at an advanced stage in the life cycle. This mentor can help the leader understand the challenges of leading in the later stages of the life cycle time and provide guidance and direction to the leader on strategies for extending their time in the role.

Leaders who are effective over an extended time frame invest in monitoring progress. They review performance metrics on a regular basis. The best leaders work this exercise into their weekly schedule. During this time, they study the metrics and reflect on the impact of their leadership on the results being produced. They ensure clarity and direct reports know their roles, their performance expectations, and how they are performing. They know the plan, their role in bringing it to life, and the status of achieving it. Leaders ensure that this happens. Metrics are important, and leaders must take responsibility for tracking progress.

> Be clear, be confident, and look for simplicity wherever possible.

Leaders must be resilient. Those effective over time have undoubtedly built up a high degree of resilience. They take time to recharge their batteries. They stay intellectually and physically active. They view mistakes as learning opportunities and always pledge to be better in the future. They keep their eyes focused forward and are not deterred by minor setbacks. They project a sense of calm and hope to others who look to them for leadership.

As highlighted earlier in the book, emotional intelligence is a key ingredient to leadership and leader success. Goleman and associates[145] suggest that there is a .85 relationship between emotional intelligence and leadership effectiveness. Leaders aspiring to excel in the leadership role and maintain their efficacy if not their role would benefit from getting professional help (e.g., conferences, online resources, coaching) in the area of emotional intelligence. Leaders who seek to be effective over an extended period of time must have passion for people, for their industry, and for leadership development.[146] It should concern leaders when their passion starts to wane in any of these areas. If they are self-aware, they will know it first. If they are not, others will soon identify it, and the leader's impact will clearly suffer.

The best leaders continually renew themselves, stay current, have an abundant level of energy, and display an unwavering passion for their field, their people, and the leadership role. When this passion fades, leadership effectiveness diminishes accordingly. If so, it is likely time to depart the role. Professor Andy Hargreaves and Dean Fink, an educational development consultant, studied the leadership practices of school principals over a period of three decades. Their research involved more than 200 teachers and administrators. Their work confirmed the work of Boyatzis and colleagues. Hargreaves and Fink, determined that top academic leaders with sustained leadership effectiveness engaged in seven practices, namely: (a) they modelled and supported continued learning; (b) they celebrated small wins and stakeholders took note; (c) they developed leadership skills in others that facilitated great leadership teams and effective leadership succession planning; (d) they were inclusive and quickly addressed any social justice issues; (e) they maximized human and material resources; (f) they built synergies where possible, and; (g) they demonstrated respect for the environment and other social causes. [147] These activities are available to most, if not all, leaders who wish to renew their leadership practices and extend their leadership shelf life. The question is whether they want to do this.

These strategies require change and investment. They can help leaders renew their leadership effectiveness and keep them in the role a bit longer. Some may wish to do this, while others may not and decide to leave the role. There is no shame in that decision, and far better for leaders to make that decision as opposed to having someone else make the decision for them. After all, all leaders do eventually leave the leadership role.

Leadership sustainability occurs when leaders not only know but feel what they should do to improve. This passion increases when leaders see their desired changes as part of their personal identities and purpose, when their changes will shape their relationships with others, and when their changes will shift the culture of their work settings.[148]

In spite of the fact that all leaders eventually leave their leadership role, and stakeholders believe that leadership matters, leaders and corporate boards don't effectively engage in succession planning. A recent Deloitte study produced results that substantiate this claim (i.e., 86% of leaders believe that leadership succession is an urgent or important priority, and only 14% that they do it well in their organization).[149] They may appreciate the fact that an effective leadership succession plan at all levels of an organization helps ensure a larger, more diverse group of potential leaders, facilitates a stronger, more cohesive organizational culture, and helps foster a greater sense of member engagement and higher retention of talent. A host of reasons why leaders and organizational stakeholders don't engage in this critical process are numerous and varied. Some may be threatened by the fact that other colleagues are being groomed for their roles. Others may seek more immediate results, and leader development takes time and results in incremental gains. Some may be looking for others to lead this program, or perhaps the content of a leadership development program is not aligned with the current and emerging needs of future leaders. Regardless of the reasons why leadership succession programs are not implemented, the importance of these programs relative to the long-term success of an organization cannot be overstated.

Identifying and developing top talent for leadership roles is crucial for organizational success.

Leaders should be focused on developing a number of others and ensure that leader development and succession planning take place throughout the organization. They need to understand the skill sets needed now, and those needed in the future. They must ensure that they select, engage, and inspire colleagues well-suited to future leadership roles. They will need to focus on the potential of people because their current roles may not allow their leadership potential to shine. They also need to be sensitive to diversity and ensure that the pipeline is filled with a diverse pool of candidates well-suited and prepared for leadership roles. This investment in people will facilitate and drive performance from better-prepared and committed colleagues who value the leader's investment in them. When the time comes, the leader will know that a number of colleagues have the background and preparation to seamlessly enter the leadership role should they be selected. The pipeline will be full of qualified internal candidates. Even if these colleagues are not selected (and naturally, some won't be if many are prepared), the organization will benefit from having more committed colleagues who have been effectively developed with heightened management and leadership skills. They will undoubtedly be prepared for leadership opportunities elsewhere.

## IMPORTANCE OF SUCCESSION PLANNING

Leaders who choose to leave on their terms typically feel good about their accomplishments and know that it was in their best interests, as well as those of the organization, for them to gracefully step aside and make room for the next leader to advance the unit. Hopefully, the organization has invested in developing leaders in the organization who can seamlessly slip into the role and maintain momentum. However, as noted above, many organizations do not have this critical process in play.

Successful transition is the last act of a great leader.
—FRANCES HESSELBEIN

Naturally, this decision requires the leader to have a high degree of self-confidence and self-awareness. Some struggle with this decision as they are unwilling to let go. As mentioned previously, they may have grown accustomed to the power, prestige, and financial rewards associated with the role. In some cases, the leader's ego won't let them relinquish the role without a fight or without making conditions difficult for their successor. Unfortunately, these types of leaders have attached their self-worth to the leadership title and often feel diminished if not in the position. Some rightfully worry about how they will fill their time when they are no longer in the leadership role. They are rudderless without occupying a leadership position. Others may not believe that anyone has the talent and experience necessary to succeed them. Those colleagues are in for a surprise.

> Leaders should always be mindful of the fact that graveyards are filled with irreplaceable leaders.

Very little has been written on this inevitable stage in the leadership life cycle. This book is one of the outliers. I suggest that leaders navigate the process. They need to view their role as a temporary stop. Hopefully, they leave the unit or organization in better shape than they found it, and they should wish that their successor does the very same thing when they leave the role.

Exiting leaders need to plan for post-leadership roles well in advance of their departure. Some may assume other leadership roles in the organization or in other organizations, some will retire from the role and adopt a quieter lifestyle. Regardless of what path departing leaders take, they need to have something to look forward to. They need a "second mountain" with new challenges and opportunities to grow. It could be in the form of a new role. It might be as a volunteer on a community board. It might be some hobbies or causes that inspire and excite the departing leader. We all need something to do, things to look forward to, and people with whom we enjoy spending time.

That said, while in the leadership role, leaders have an obligation to create other leaders. They need to ensure that colleagues have excellent supervision, meaningful feedback on their performance, and plentiful opportunities to develop and refine their leadership skills. They need to create more leaders.

Marshall Goldsmith is a rare example of a writer who provides guidance to those at or near the end of the leadership lifecycle. His small but impactful book entitled *Succession: Are you ready?*[150] is one of the few sources available to leaders hoping to effectively navigate this stage in the leadership lifecycle. In his book, Goldsmith helps leaders better understand how to come to terms with the inevitable departure from the role and why so many leaders struggle with the process. Great leaders know when it is time to go. They understand the need for change in themselves and in the unit they lead. They may need new challenges or, as David Brooks[151] suggests in his insightful book, a fresh mountain to climb.

Researchers[152] have shown that leadership succession is an important strategic process for leaders and the organizations they lead. The best leaders ensure that a number of potential successors have the experience and development opportunities to succeed the leader. I believe that a leader will surround themselves with higher quality leaders if they know that their leader will invest in their development. As a result, I wish that more organizations hired leaders from within who have demonstrated their commitment and developed themselves to be strong and viable candidates for succession.

> Studies indicate that internally cultivated leaders promoted from within the organization generate higher rates of organizational performance than externally recruited counterparts. Consideration for internal promotion is supported by other studies that have shown that organizations that place an emphasis on in-house promotion report higher financial returns than those organizations that did not.[153]

However, a fact of organizational life is that the best leaders are not afraid to make decisions, and some of these decisions will disappoint some people. External candidates make the same decisions in their current settings, but they are generally not known to those making the hiring decision. Organizations and those who lead them should be concerned. They need to develop future leaders, and in my opinion, engage in strategic succession planning activities. Organizations need to be more open to internal promotions as opposed to automatically believing someone from outside the organization will be better qualified to lead the unit. In addition, they will know what they are getting with internal candidates because they have worked with these people for many years. They will know their strengths and areas of challenge. They may not fully understand the ceiling of these candidates because they may not have had the opportunity to lead as much in their current roles. That is why job rotations, acting positions, and secondments make sense as part of the leader development process. Internal appointments also make sense for candidates who can adapt quickly and know exactly what they are getting into. Decision-makers should not be fooled by a charismatic candidate from the outside who interviews well, may not authentically have the right skill set, and often comes at a higher cost (e.g., search firm cost, salary and relocation demands). Developing leaders from within will help ensure continuity and momentum (assuming the organization is performing well), and it sends a strong message that the organization values their own people.

> Leaders have an obligation to throw the ladder down and help the next generation of leaders develop and emerge.

Once a successor has been named, the leader needs to play an active role in onboarding the new leader in a seamless manner so the new leader hits the ground running. If leaders truly care about their unit or organization and the people left behind, they should do everything in their power to help the next leader and the organization succeed. They need to transfer information to the new leader and provide them with their assessment of the opportunities and challenges. They need to help them develop relationships with key stakeholders in the unit and across the organization or industry. They need to help the new leader succeed. Many don't. In fact, some are so threatened by the new leader that they throw them an anchor instead, and it sinks them!!!

> Succession planning is the process of identifying and preparing suitable employees through mentoring, coaching, and job rotation to replace key organizational members as their tenures come to an end, usually through retirement, resignation, and other factors.[154]

Jim Collins and Jerry Porras noted in their best-selling book *Built to last: Successful habits of visionary companies* that the key to success for the best organizations is their investment in leader development and succession planning. Organizations that do this well commit resources to the process and ensure that succession planning takes place at all levels of the organization. This commitment helps "build the bench" of engaged and progressive leaders who are more effective in their current roles, more committed to the organization, and prepared for subsequent opportunities when they become available. Ineffective organizations rely too heavily on single leaders, and their leadership succession plans are best described as crisis-driven and leading to predictably poor outcomes. Ineffective leaders in these types of organizations often feel the need to hang on to the roles long after the "best before date" because they or others feel that no one is ready or capable of replacing them. Truth be told, this predicament is actually the fault of leaders not insisting on a focused leadership development program and a conceptually strong leadership succession plan for all levels of the organization.

In some cases, leaders play an active role in choosing their successors. Other times they have no input or involvement. There are strengths and weaknesses to each approach. Goldsmith covers those areas in his insightful book. In higher education, leaders are usually consulted about the challenges and opportunities facing their successor but usually have little or no input in the selection process.

Leaders should always be focused on developing other leaders and preparing them for opportunities. To me, it is a prerequisite of being a leader.

> The job of as leader is not to create followers. It's to create more leaders.
>
> —RALPH NADAR

Regardless of whether organizations have formal succession programs in place, the best leaders prepare members of their team for opportunities within the host organization or other organizations. They serve as role models, mentor and coach team members, and advocate for them where warranted and appropriate. They open doors of opportunity for their colleagues, and they ensure that they are prepared to succeed in new leadership opportunities. It is my feeling that leaders attract higher quality people who know that they will learn new skills, gain valuable experience, have responsibility and authority, and perhaps, have opportunities for advancement in the future. Think of the coaching trees of successful football coaches like Nick Saban in the NCAA, Bill Belichick in the National Football League or Greg Marshall in Canadian University Football. All three of these coaches have produced an inordinate number of coaches who are now head coaches in their respective leagues. These protégé head coaches credit the knowledge, experience, and support they received from their mentor coaches as being critical to their career advancement.

While internally developed and promoted leaders might be able to "hit the ground running" faster than externally appointed leaders, all new leaders should participate in a conceptually strong onboarding process.

The best onboarding strategies provide a fast-track to meaningful, productive work and strong employee relationships. Onboarding programs – the acquiring, accommodating, assimilating, and accelerating of new leaders into an organizational culture and business – need to be tailored specifically to the needs of the organization and the individuals. [155]

# IMPORTANCE OF STRATEGIC ONBOARDING

Researchers have documented the fact that 30-40% of executive leaders fail within the first 18 months in their new position.[156] What a shame. Some suggest that there may be a cultural mismatch not detected in the interview. Others point to a failure of new leaders to build and nurture necessary relationships with key stakeholders. Still others point to leaders not understanding key processes or being influenced by the wrong people. Ross and colleagues[157] suggest that a conceptually strong and effectively implemented onboarding program would help minimize these negative impacts. Readers and leaders should look to Goldsmith[158] for insightful advice on onboarding new leaders and helping set things up for their success and guard against a derailment. Unfortunately, typical onboarding programs lack a conceptual plan and are often more social than productive.[159] Onboarding programs should include five elements, namely: (a) understanding the unit and its strengths, weaknesses, past successes, and areas of challenge; (b) a clear understanding of the incoming leader's key performance indicators and expectations; (c) a strategy to get the leader assimilated to the culture of the organization; (d) a process to help the leader understand the readiness of the unit to change and a plan to inspire change (See Kotter[160]), and; (e) helping the new leader build relationships with his or her leadership team and key stakeholders across the organization.

Goldsmith agrees and suggests that exiting leaders should ensure that the incoming leader has met the key people, understands the challenges and opportunities that lie ahead, and knows that they can reach out for input if needed.

> A well-designed and coordinated onboarding process assimilates new employees into the organization and equips them with the tools and resources needed for professional and personal success.[161]

## SUPPORT BUT GET OUT OF THE WAY

Outgoing leaders need to let go and be sure that they do not bind their successors with personnel or financial commitment that could negatively impact their success. I have onboarded new leaders on a few occasions and always offer the caveat that I am happy to share my experiences and observations if they want them and that I fully expect them to lead things their way. I know that they will make decisions differently than those that I made. I expect that some of the strategies and activities that were important to me will not be priorities for the new leader. I remind myself that I always did the same when I entered a new leadership position. Incoming leaders can benefit from an existing leader who is committed to them and helping them get off to a good start. Colleagues often look to an outgoing leader for their impressions of an incoming leader. Take the high road – always. Be positive and supportive. Be available for phone calls or visits that might help the incoming leader, but keep a distance, and be especially mindful of the debilitating impact the "good old days" comments can have on the incoming leader's impact. Colleagues may need to be reminded that they have a new leader who needs their support now.

Finding the right balance of engagement is critical and sometimes tricky. Some incoming leaders want to hear from former leaders and hear their insights, suggestions, and offers of assistance. Others want a clean break. Regardless, it is important that exiting leaders give new leaders the support and space to assume the leadership role. Many find this to be easier said than done. Some hang around, and their presence impairs the incoming leader's ability to assume the mantle of leadership. After all, the purpose of the onboarding activities is for the exiting leader to move and the incoming leader to have the information, contacts, and support necessary to flatten the learning curve. Leaders can help their successors by making difficult decisions before the successor arrives. Ineffective leaders ignore issues and push them on to their successors. Great leaders make tough decisions that have to be made and free their successor to enter the role with a clean slate and more positive activities to engage in initially.

Goldsmith covers the topic with compassion for these people, as he is sensitive to the personal feelings, fears, and anxieties associated with leaving roles that leaders cherish, through which they identify themselves, and in most cases, that they often worked so hard to attain. Like a few others (e.g., David Brooks[162]), Goldsmith is an outlier as a writer in this critical and inevitable area. Those reading his book, as well as this one, can gain valuable insights that will help them look ahead and do so with pride and excitement, leaving the role with their dignity intact.

People who advance to a senior leadership role are usually task-oriented people who love to be busy. They have made many sacrifices along the way and have worked hard to earn and excel in the role. Unfortunately, many identify themselves through this role. It becomes who they are. Consequently, leaving the role can be painful if there is nothing that outgoing leaders can look forward to doing. However, leaving the role with people wanting more should be a leader's wish. As well, departing leaders should want the next leader to be successful so the organization and colleagues can succeed. The best leaders do this well and always ensure that the group or organization is set up for sustained success and prosperity.

## ENSURING A SMOOTH TRANSITION

Leadership transitions can be very disruptive. It takes time for the new leader to adjust to their new surroundings. Relationships need to be forged, and they take time. Leaders often need to understand new systems and the formal and informal networks and communication channels. Outgoing leaders can shorten this adjustment period for new leaders by effectively onboarding them. Effective onboarding strategies and practices are outlined later in this chapter. Ideally, the transition should be smooth and seamless, and new leaders can effectively hit the ground running. Goldsmith[163] extends this metaphor by comparing the leadership transition process to a relay race. Olympic-calibre relay team members have trained hard to prepare themselves individually and collectively to compete. All members have a single goal in mind, and everyone is committed to the success of the team. Like a leader, a relay runner moves at full speed and effectively hands the baton to the next runner (i.e., leader) who is running at top speed when the baton is passed (i.e., just like a new leader who is carefully developed, selected, and onboarded to ensure immediate impact). Like the relay team, the organization or unit does not have to slow down during this period of transition. Great relay teams exchange the baton with both runners moving at peak speed. Although Goldsmith doesn't make this point, the metaphor could be extended because the new runner (i.e., the new leader) will eventually pass the baton to the person (i.e., the next leader) who succeeds them. The chain continues, and speed or momentum does not need to be sacrificed.

## GRACEFUL EXIT AND MOVING ON TO THE NEXT MOUNTAIN

Outgoing leaders often comment that their impact will diminish once the new leader is named. This is a reality of organizational life. Superiors and decision-makers are generally unwilling to make commitments to the outgoing leader and or the unit, preferring to wait until the new leader is installed so commitments can be evaluated by them on the basis of strategic fit. Some outgoing leaders worry that they might become a "lame duck", and according to Goldsmith[164], they will become one. However, as he wisely suggests, leaders can shift their focus and, in doing so, help the incoming leader even more. It won't be long before the outgoing leader has to introduce him or herself at the reception desk of the organization he or she used to lead. Staff change. People won't know you or your impact. It is part of the transition period.

They should consider this phenomenon to be a natural part of the transition process. Goldsmith suggests that those who manage this transition effectively actively engage their successors in decisions, make tough calls to help the incoming leader manage relationships, and, remind colleagues how excited they are for the future of the group under the influence of the incoming leader. This approach will help the organization, and some outgoing leaders take great pride in how they positively manage the transition.

One thing is certain - outgoing leaders need to get out of the way of the incoming leader. Their time in the role is passed, and it is time for the new leader to establish his or her identity as the leader of the unit. Move on. Find new challenges. Support the new leader by being available for a call or Zoom chat, but physically remove yourself. Do all you can to put your successor in a position where they can succeed.

Outgoing leaders often feel neglected after they leave. Some report being disappointed that that the organization turned too quickly to the successor. Get used to it. That is part of the transition process. The organization has moved on and so should you. Let the unit throw a party for you in your honour but know that the honour will be short-lived. It is time for you and the organization to move on. Be proud of what you accomplished and let go of grudges or regrets. Take comfort in knowing that you did the best you could. Be proud of your accomplishments but look ahead, not back. Hopefully you can watch colleagues continue to soar in their careers, but your time as the leader of that group is over. Move on. Let go. Refocus.

Outgoing leaders are generally high-energy people who also need something to look forward to doing. Some may decide to move into new roles in the organization that challenge them. Some may leave the organization and find challenges in civic engagement or exciting new volunteer roles. Either way, outgoing leaders have lots to offer and generally need another mountain to climb to assist them in the transition. One of my mentors was Richard Peddie, the former CEO and President of Maple Leaf Sports and Entertainment in Canada. He led this organization, arguably Canada's top sport organization, for many years. He was in the print and electronic media constantly. He wanted to do something quite different at this stage in his life – and he did. He and his wife moved to a small town and opened a bookshop, kitchen store, and candy shop. Another colleague of mine joined a number of boards outside her academic area. These gave her a chance to learn new skills, develop a new leadership network, and make a difference in her community. Another retired leader I know went back to school and is doing a graduate degree in a field completely outside of his professional expertise and previous career. Another colleague went completely off plan and joined a Rock and Roll band.

Outgoing leaders generally want to contribute to something important to them, and in many ways, they need to be engaged in something meaningful that helps them fill their day. Leadership is a social process, and these outgoing leaders need to do things with other people. They need mental stimulation, social networks, and the satisfaction of knowing that they are doing something meaningful at this stage in their lives and following their leadership tenures. As well, it goes without saying that they usually have a great deal of experience and skill to make meaningful contributions to new areas. According to Goldsmith,[165] being active, assuming challenging assignments, and feeling like one is continuing to contribute helps eases the transition for existing leaders.

"Move on and create a great rest of your life."[166]
— MARSHALL GOLDSMITH

Earlier in the book, I covered the undeniable role that role models, mentors, and sponsors can have on leader development and on the way up. Leaders can effectively use role models, mentors and sponsors to help them through the exiting process as well. As noted, all leaders go through it at one point or another.

Follow the lead of former leaders who effectively transitioned. Meet with them and ask them how they navigated the process. Learn from their experiences and try to emulate those who have done it well. Perhaps they implemented strategies that would also work for you. Talk to these people about their feelings after they navigated the process. Ask them what you might expect to feel. What were their concerns, and how did they manage them? What strategies did they put in place? What might they do differently if given the opportunity?

You will undoubtedly hear about the need to make a clean break. Leadership roles are temporary. Hopefully, you can take pride in the fact that the unit is in better shape now than it was when you entered the role. Be proud of that accomplishment but move on. Those who have done this well will undoubtedly counsel outgoing leaders to look ahead. Depending on career stage, some might be headed into new roles or challenges. Others may welcome a nice break and the found time to pursue other interests. Regardless of the end focus, outgoing leaders need to get out of the way of the next leader. Your presence alone can be a distraction for colleagues, and the new leader needs the space and profile to carve their own identity and forge their leadership agenda. Leaders who hang around can be a distraction and actually hurt the organization. Some may hope that they will rise from the dead and return. Some may wish to seek a former leader's opinion on a new strategy or decision. It is inappropriate and counterproductive to stay involved. Onboarding the new leader effectively before he or she takes over will help them meet colleagues and understand the critical issues, but the former leader needs to subsequently back away.

Colleagues will undoubtedly come to the former leader to reminisce about "days gone by" or make a negative comment about the new leader. Former leaders would be well-served in "nipping these situations in the bud" by reminding colleagues that the new leader needs their support and that they actually honour you by giving the new leader the same level of commitment and support. The new leader may have questions and should know that they can always engage in a quick Zoom call or phone chat if they wish. However, many outgoing leaders struggle with "getting their hands off the rudder." It is not your ship anymore. It is why having a new ship to steer (e.g., a new position or other personal goals) will help facilitate this transition.

## SUMMARY

Like fruit, meat, and medicine, leaders also have a best-before date, and the reality is that every leader will eventually leave the role. Some recognize the signs and signal that their influence is waning, and they reinvent themselves and effectively extend their shelf life. Others decide that leaving the leader role and moving on to other interests and challenges is the better option. Still others don't have the self-awareness or instincts to know that change is required, and others make the decision for them. These scenarios happen far too frequently and are painful and disruptive for all parties. They can be avoided. However, to date, few leadership scholars have focused on this area. Departing leaders turning to the literature for advice on this inevitable practice will find that very little exists. Readers can find countless sources to help them excel in the role. Far fewer can be found on leader development and even less on the inevitable departure stage. This book was prepared to help fill that void.

There are "blue ribbon" indicators that change is needed, either in the leader or of the leader. Perhaps their passion for the role has diminished. They may not listen as acutely as they once did. Perhaps they rely too much on their experience and instincts when they need to be more open to new ideas and perspectives. Perhaps they have not kept up with developments in their field, and it will be hard for them to catch up. Finally, they may have concluded that they completed what they set out to do, and it is time for a new leader to assume the reins and springboard the unit or organization forward. Regardless of the reason, the fact remains that all leaders leave the role. This book was designed to help leaders understand how to effectively navigate the process for their good, as well as for the benefit of their organization. Great leaders have developed a number of colleagues and prepared them for future leadership roles. They may succeed the leader, or they may not. Regardless, a leader's responsibility is to develop team members so they can, and in doing so, give the organization viable options for succession. In addition to succession planning, great leaders can help their successors "hit the ground" running by effectively onboarding their successors. They ensure that their successor has access to the relevant information, meets the key stakeholders before starting, and is presented in a positive fashion. Ineffective, and I might add, insecure leaders withhold information, keep incoming leaders away from stakeholders, and talk negatively about their successors, perhaps as a way of boosting their old image or hoping that they might be resurrected to "save" the unit or organization.

Some leaders effectively transition themselves and their organization, and some do it poorly. The reality is that everyone will do it at some point. This chapter is designed to provide leaders with the tools to do it well, for their benefit, for their successor's benefit, for the benefit of organization, and for the benefit of the people the leader is leaving behind.

# CONCLUSION

## A READER'S GUIDE:

Upon reading this Chapter readers will understand:

- ○ the genesis and test marking of the leadership lifecycle concept;
- ○ the reaction of audience members at all stages of the leadership life cycle, and;
- ○ my genuine desire that the book and its contents will make a difference for those seeking leadership roles, those in leadership roles, and those preparing to exit leadership roles.

As noted in the introduction, the genesis of this book came from the three most repeated questions or comments that I receive when I am at speaking engagements or book signings. I am amazed at the frequency with which these questions emerged. I reflected deeply on them before embarking on this book project. Audience members sought precise and helpful responses. These people have prompted me to delve into the research literature and the popular press. Yes, I found some content on leader and leadership development, mostly in academic journals that rarely worked its way into the hands and minds of younger colleagues and students seeking practical information on how they could prepare for future leadership roles that they hoped would come available. I found lots of research and gray literature on how to excel in the leadership role, but I thought that I could simplify and demystify the advice and repackage it into the six practices outlined in Part 2 of the book. I hope that this end has been met. What really stood out for me was the relative dearth of information related to departing the role. What are the signs and signals that a leader's influence is waning? What steps can they take to regain their influential role, and when it is time to depart, how can they do it with grace and dignity as well as leaving the unit or organization with a strong stable of well-prepared leaders and an onboarding program that facilitates future success? I found a few sources on succession planning and some on onboarding. However, I found very little in effectively departing the role, and especially doing so on the leader's schedule.

As per my practice, I put together a leadership presentation on the topic, and due to the success of *The 5C Leader* book, I found my way to the podiums of corporate retreats, service clubs, and university campuses where I have shared my model and gauged the reaction of those in the audience. My test marking of my concept, entitled "The Leadership Lifecycle" (i.e., How to get on? How to excel? When (and how) to exit?) seemed to resonate with audience members at all ages and career stages. I could see heads bobbing as I went through the content. Some of the heads were senior leaders who were hungry for information on the latter stage of the lifecycle model. Many saw themselves in my examples and could personally identify with the content. Based on the comments of these colleagues, many were interested in effectively extending their time in the role. They seemed to like the suggestions and recognized the need for them to engage in revitalization strategies outlined in this book. Still, others have indicated that they are thinking about their pending departure and they are worried about themselves and what they might do. They seemed to be comforted by the obvious fact that all leaders eventually go through this process, and they appeared to value the strategies to ensure a smooth transition for them and their organization. Some picked up on the succession planning suggestions that are outlined in the book and admitted that they needed to do more on that front. Others pointed to the onboarding advice and hoped to implement the strategies that are outlined in this book.

Some of those in attendance have been mid-career leaders who want to extend their leadership impact and engage in practices allowing them to maintain their impact and extend their lifecycle. A few have admitted that they felt that they were becoming stale and needed to recharge. They recognized the signs and signals of decline but they were confident that they could recapture their impact by engaging in the practices outlined in the session and in the book. The six practices seemed to make sense to them. Many have quietly admitted to me that could do more to advance practice number six and they committed to engaging, modelling, and supporting a more robust program of learning and regular reflection.

The final group that I have identified in my audiences were students or younger colleagues who envisioned senior leadership roles in their futures. I loved their ambition and enthusiasm. Always have, and always will. It was my prime motivation for embarking on a career as a university professor and academic leader. I witnessed in these audience members a genuine interest and authentic passion for the content. They would come to the front of the room following the session to tell me of their plans and activities or seek specific advice and direction about their journey. They were keen and willing to listen. I felt that they were ready to put these practices into play. Specifically, they wanted answers on what they could do to better prepare themselves for opportunities that they hoped would lie ahead. They wanted to learn more about how they could prepare themselves, and effectively position themselves for future leadership roles in their chosen field. I was excited for them. In many ways, I often felt like I was speaking to a younger version of myself.

I have found the reactions of these audience members, and the follow-up questions that they posed, to be invigorating and it was clear to me that that I was on to something different with the leadership lifecycle concept. It was time for me to return to my writer's garret and get to work on crafting a leadership book that would make a difference. *The Leadership Lifecycle: How to Get On, How to Excel, and When, (and How) to Effectively Exit* quickly came together.

## THROWING DOWN THE LADDER – MY "RE-GIFT" TO YOU

I completed my undergraduate degree in 1980 and in the senior years of the program I encountered a professor who changed my life. His lectures were captivating, stories of his life experiences were riveting. I decided then and there that I wanted to follow in his footsteps and be just like him. Having read this book you would understand that he was a role model for me, and later became a strong mentor and sponsor. Emulating him was not enough. I needed a Master's Degree, a doctoral degree, and a record of accomplishment in the teaching and research areas if that was going to happen. I applied to the Master's program and Bob agreed to take me on as his first graduate student. I started my graduate program and kickstarted my journey into higher education. I tried to "hit the ground running", but in doing so I may have displayed too much enthusiasm.

I recall meeting Bob for an early advisory meeting. He must have felt that I needed a bit more balance and he introduced me to Richard's Bolles' *The Three Boxes of Life and How to Get Out of Them* book that has been a blueprint for my life, and one that I have shared with generations of students. I firmly believe it has great utility for effectively navigating The Leadership Lifecycle.

Bolles suggests that people typically live their lives in one of three boxes (i.e., box of education, box of work, box of retirement). He notes that people are unusually fully immersed in one of these three boxes as they move through life stages, often looking forward to the next box until they realize that the box that they were in had its benefits. He flips the paradigm and suggests that we should seek more balances across the boxes (e.g., when in the box of education, also get work experiences and develop hobbies that you find interesting; when the in the box of work keep taking courses and engage in professional development activities but be sure to continue to develop and refine your outside interests; when in the box of retirement continue to take courses and learn new things, assume volunteer and part-time work experiences and pursue your hobbies and interests).

I firmly believe that this approach will help leaders develop, excel, and effectively navigate the *Leadership Life Cycle*. The adjustments will not be so drastic or disruptive. As a student I continued to play hockey and golf. While in my career I became a coach of my children's teams, learned to play the guitar, developed an interest in gardening, and developed an appreciation for art and art history. As I enter the box of retirement, I have set my sights on learning to play the piano, playing more hockey, golf, and guitar, volunteering with a number of organizations and Board, and spending more time with my family, my friends and my former colleagues. The transition will not be as challenging due to adopting the principles in the Bolles' book on my way through life. I adopted the practices outlined in the book that my mentor shared with me over 40 years ago. I hope that they serve you just as well.

Thanks Bob.

I hope that you have enjoyed reading the book, can see the relevance and application, and that the content makes a difference for you. I have certainly enjoyed putting it together. Now get after it.

Lead on my friend!!!

> There is nothing more difficult to take in hand, more perilous to conduct, or more uncertain in its success, than to take the lead in the introduction of a new order of things.
>
> —MACHIAVELLI

# APPENDIX A

## WESTERN UNIVERSITY

**Western Leader Academy**

**What:**

- An intense program designed to develop the next generation of academic leaders
- Six full-day sessions; meetings, small group activities, preparation and stretch assignments in between the sessions
- Focused on both the development of management and leadership skills
- Focus on contemporary issues/needs (e.g., leading/managing in the age of: information overload, intergenerational issues, need to differentiate, need for interconnectedness, innovation, leading change, age of technological change, globalization, advancing research, etc).
- Burning Issues segments will allow us to focus on the current and anticipated scenarios facing academic leaders.

**How:**

- A highly interactive/deep schedule of learning activities that include (but not limited to): mini-lectures, small group activities, readings/assignments, diagnostics, panel presentations, 360's, guest speakers, role-playing, case studies, 1-1 meetings, follow up coaching
- Application activities, individual and working groups will be interspersed in the times between the group sessions
- Guided discussion circles will follow each module so members can reflect on the material, discuss its utility and application

## Skelton Outline

**Group Meeting Date #1 Theme:**
**On the Path to Excellent Academic Leadership**

- How to get the most out of the Western Leader Academy
- Academic Leadership Lessons and Insights from our President
- Your Leadership Style and Tendencies
- Why Strong Leadership is Critical to Western's Success: Provost's Perspectives
- Insights and Experiences Academic Leaders
- Alignment – how the Western Leader Academy fits into Western's Leader Development Programs
- Case Studies, *Activities*, Burning Issues, Deep Dives/ Reflections

**Meeting Date #2 Theme:**
**Future Proofing Higher Education: The Role of the Academic Leader**

- Leader's Role in Future-Proofing our Institution/Higher Education
- Linking Strategy and Risk Adverse Leadership

- Academic Leadership in a Post Pandemic Era
- Character and Academic Leadership
- Role Models, Mentors and Sponsors: How benefitted/how to help others
- Case Studies, Activities, Burning Issues, Deep Dives/ Reflections

**Meeting Date #3 Theme:**
**A Team Approach to Academic Leadership**

- Book Review/Presentation – *The Five Dysfunctions of a Team*
- A Team Approach to Academic Leadership
- The Ideal Team Player
- Ensuring Equity, Diversity and Inclusion (EDI)
- What Units can do you ensure EDI
- Leadership and Emotional Intelligence
- Engaging Introverts
- Building and Earning Trust
- Engagement and a Decision-Making Exercise
- Case Studies, Activities, Burning Issues, Deep Dives/Reflections

**Meeting Date #4 Theme:**
**Ensuring a Clear Strategic Focus/Aligning Resources and Budget**

- Book Review/Presentation – *Leading Change*
- Strategic Reviews: Process, Role and Function
- Aligning Budget and Strategy
- Staff Support: Role Clarity
- Campus Alignment
- Case Studies, Activities, Burning Issues, Deep Dives/ Reflections

**Meeting Date #5 Themes:**
**(a) Management and Leadership Skills for Contemporary Academic Leaders**

(b) **The Leadership Life Cycle: Effectively Securing, Excelling, and Exiting the Leadership Role**

- Paper Review/Presentation – *Essential Academic Leadership Practices that Facilitate Success (and Survival)*
- Formal and Informal Communication Strategies and Processes
- Project Management
- Fostering and Advancing Innovation
- Meeting Management
- Alumni and Development
- Government and Community Relations
- Managing Conflict and Conflict Resolution
- Preparing for Academic Leadership
- Insights from Search Consultants: Interview Tips and Traps
- The Leadership Life Cycle:
- Case Studies, Burning Issues, Deep Dives/Reflections

**Meeting Date #6 Theme:**
**Pulling it All Together: Springboard to Success in Academic Leadership**

- Book Review/Presentations: The 5C Leader: Exceptional Leadership Practices for Extraordinary Times
- Advancing Western's Strategic Priorities: Role of Academic Leaders
- Staying Healthy and Productive: Insights from Long Serving Leaders
- Driving Transformation
- Dare to Lead
- Case Studies, Activities, Burning Issues, Deep Dives/ Reflections
- Graduation Reception and Future Commitments

# NOTES

## Gear 1 - The Preparation Phase

1   Bowness, A. (2017). Five ways to develop great leaders. *Strategic HR Review.* *16*(4), 189-191

2   See Bass, B. M. (1990). *Bass and Stogdill's handbook of leadership: Theory, research and managerial applications.* New York: Free Press, or one of Bennis, W. G., & Thomas, R. J. (2007). *Leading for a lifetime.* Boston, MA: Harvard Business School Publishing or Bennis, W., & Ward Biederman, P. (2010). *Still surprized: A memoir of a life in leadership.* Jossey-Bass.

3   Readers are encouraged to read the work of Warren Bennis, and especially Bennis W. (2009). *On becoming leader: The leadership classic.* The geopolitical events and social divide he describes in 2009 have significantly worsened. His call for more collaborative leaders who employ abundant levels of integrity and empathy seems to be more true today than they were when he clairvoyantly echoed them in 2009. The leadership practices outlined in the middle section of this book call for these types of emotionally-intelligent leaders who are honest, trustworthy, welcome dissenting opinions, and leaders who never stop learning. It is a call to action for those hoping to be effective in the role. This portion of the book will help readers get there so they can lead that way.

4    The late-great Bernard Bass devoted an entire chapter (35) to the "born or made" debate in his comprehensive text. Readers seeking an historical overview of the theoretical developments in the area of leadership are encouraged to read Bass, B. M. (1990). *Bass and Stogdill's handbook of leadership: Theory, research and managerial applications*. New York: Free Press.

5    Hernez-Broome, G., & Hughes, R. J., (2004). Leadership development: Past, present, and future. *Human Resource Planning, 27*(1), 24-32. (p. 27)

6    Chaturvedi, S., Zyphur, M. J., Arvey, R. D., Avolio, B. J. & Larsson, G. (2012). The heritability of emergent leadership: Age and gender as moderating factors. *The Leadership Quarterly, 23*(2), 219-232. https://doi.org/10.1016/j.leaqua.2011.08.004.

7    Arvey, R. D., Rotundo, M., Johnson, W., Zhang, Z., & McGue, M. (2006). The determinants of leadership role occupancy: Genetic and personality factors, *The Leadership Quarterly, 17*(1), 1-20, https://doi.org/10.1016/j.leaqua.2005.10.009.

8    Arvey, R. D., Zhang, Z., Avolio, B. J., & Krueger, R. F. (2007). Developmental and genetic determinants of leadership role occupancy among women. *Journal of Applied Psychology, 92*(3), 693–706. https://doi.org/10.1037/0021-9010.92.3.693

9    Gentry, W., Deal, J. J., Stawiski, S., & Ruderman, M. (2012). Are leaders born or made. *Center for Creative Leadership, 2*(1).

10   Zhang, Z., Ilies, R., & Avery, R.D. (2009). Beyond genetic explanations for leadership: The moderating role of the social environment. *Organizational Behavior and Human Decision Processes, 110*(2), 118-128 https://doi.org/10.1016/j.obhdp.2009.06.004.

11   Barling, J., & Weatherhead, J. G. (2016). Persistent exposure to poverty during childhood limits later leader emergence. *Journal of Applied Psychology, 101*(9), 1305, and Zhang, Z., Ilies, R., & Arvey, R. D. (2009). Beyond genetic explanations for leadership: The moderating role of the social environment. *Organizational Behavior and Human Decision Processes, 110*(2), 118-128.

12   Schultz, N. L. (1993). Leadership: Effects of birth order and education. *Nursing Management, 24*(8), 4. Retrieved from https://www.lib.uwo.ca/cgi-bin/ezpauthn.cgi?url=http://search.proquest.com/scholarly-journals/leadership-effects-birth-order-education/docview/231404411/se-2?accountid=15115

      Readers would also find support for this claim in the research of Yaremych, H. E., & Volling, B. L. (2020). Sibling relationships and mothers' and fathers' emotion socialization practices: A within-family perspective. *Early Child Development and Care, 190*(2), 195-209.

13  Readers are encouraged to read the insightful for of Hardy, R. C., Hunt, J., & Lehr, E. (1978). Relationship between birth order and leadership style for nursery school children. *Perceptual and Motor Skills, 46*(1), 184-186.

14  Ibid

15  Readers are encouraged to read the insightful book by David Foot (Foot, D. K. (1996). *Boom, bust and echo: How to profit from the coming demographic shift.* Macfarland, Walter & Ross) to gain a better understanding of the strong and powerful impact of demographics and their impact on everything from opportunity, competition, marketplace shifts, the economy, and employment opportunities. His work is also helpful in explaining the abundance or dearth of leadership opportunities for generations of people.

16  Fulghum, R. (1986). *All I Really Needed to Know I Learned in Kindergarten: Uncommon Thoughts on Common Things. Ballantine Books.*

17  See Day, D. V., & Dragoni, L. (2015). Leadership development: An outcome-oriented review based on time and levels of analyses. *Annual Review of Organizational Psychology and Organizational Behavior, 2*(1) 133-156.

18  Brungardt, C. (1996). The making of leaders: A review of the research in leadership development and education. *Journal of Leadership Studies, 3*(3), 81-95.

19  Oliver, P. H., Gottfried, A. W., Guerin, D. W., Gottfried, A. E., Reichard, R. J., & Riggio, R. E. (2011). Adolescent family environmental antecedents to transformational leadership potential: A longitudinal mediational analysis. *The Leadership Quarterly, 22*(3), 535-544.

20  Liu, L., Wang, N., & Tian, L. (2019). The parent-adolescent relationship and risk-taking behaviors among Chinese adolescents: the moderating role of self-control. *Frontiers in Psychology, 10*(542), 1-8. https://doi.org/10.3389/fpsyg.2019.00542

21  Readers are encouraged to review the work of Hancock, D., Dyk, P. H., & Jones, K. (2012). Adolescent involvement in extracurricular activities: influences on leadership skills. *Journal of Leadership Education, 11*(1).

22  Readers should review the work of Reitan, T., & Stenberg, S. Å. (2019). From classroom to conscription. Leadership emergence in childhood and early adulthood. *The Leadership Quarterly, 30*(3), 298-319 as well as that of Atwater, L. E., Dionne, S. D., Avolio, B., Camobreco, J. E., & Lau, A. W. (1999). A longitudinal study of the leadership development process:

Individual differences predicting leader effectiveness. *Human relations,* *52*(12), 1543-1562.

23 See Weese, W.J. (2018). *The 5C leader: Exceptional leadership practices for* *extraordinary times.* New York: Archway Publishing, a Division of Simon and Schuster or visit https://www.5cleader.com/

24 Ayman, R., Adams, S., Fisher, B., & Hartman, E. (2003). Leadership development in higher education institutions: A present and future perspective. The future of leadership development, 201-222 and Riggio, R. E., Ciulla, J. B., & Sorenson, G. J. (2003). Leadership education at the undergraduate level: A liberal arts approach to leadership development. In S. E. Murphy & R. E. Riggio (Eds.), *The future of leadership development* (249-262). Psychology Press. https://doi.org/10.4324/9781410608895

25 Fulmer, R. M., Gibbs, P. A., & Goldsmith, M. (2000). Developing leaders: How winning companies keep on winning. *MIT Sloan Management* *Review, 42*(1), 49-59. (p. 49)

26 Ibid

27 Sternberg, R. J. (2011). Leadership and education: Leadership stories. In *Leadership studies.* Edward Elgar Publishing.

28 Beard, S., & Weese, W. J. (2020). A 50-year retrospective of leadership development through varsity sport from the former athletes' perspective. *Journal for the Study of Sports and Athletics in Education,* 1-25. doi.org/10. 1080/19357397.2020.1774238

29 Emotional intelligence (EQ) is the single most important concept that I teach in my leadership classes and in mentoring sessions with current and aspiring leaders. According to Goleman (2005). *Emotional intelligence:* *Why it can matter more than IQ.* Bantam Books, emotional intelligence is critical to connecting with others and to leadership success. Readers (and especially those interested in heightening their preparation for leadership and subsequent leader effectiveness are encouraged to read the transformative work of scholars like Goleman, Boytatzis, McKee, and Nadler.

30 Goleman, D. (2019). *The emotionally intelligent leader.* Harvard Business Review Press and Goleman, D., Boyatzis, R., & McKee, A. (2013). *Primal* *leadership: Realizing the power of emotional intelligence.* Harvard Business School Press.

31 Ibid

32 Ibid

33 The 5C Leadership scale is introduced in Weese, W. J. (2018). *The 5C* *Leader: Exceptional leadership practices for extraordinary times,* and can be accessed at: https://www.5cleader.com/

34  Researchers have demonstrated that "other" measures are typically the most valid assessments (as opposed to self-assessments) and the "other" measures more favourably correlate to the most popular outcome measures of leadership research (i.e., member satisfaction and organizational effectiveness). Readers are encouraged to review Weese, W. J. (2001). Are sport management executive leaders as good as they think? *The European Journal for Sport Management, 7*, 2, 65-76 for additional information on this area.

35  Readers would benefit from reviewing the insightful work of Liu, Z., Venkatesh, S., Murphy, S. E., & Riggio, R. E. (2021). Leader development across the lifespan: A dynamic experiences-grounded approach. *The Leadership Quarterly, 32*(5). doi.org/10.1016/j.leaqua.2020.101382.

36  Readers are encouraged to read the insightful work of Goleman, D. (2019). *The emotionally intelligent leader.* Harvard Business Review Press and Goleman, D., Boyatzis, R., & McKee, A. (2013). *Primal leadership: Realizing the power of emotional intelligence.* Harvard Business School Press.

37  Weese, W. J. (2018). *The 5C Leader: Exceptional leadership practices for extraordinary times,* and can be accessed at: https://www.5cleader.com/

38  Readers are referred to Crossan, M., Seijts, G., & Gandz, J. (2015). *Developing leadership character.* Routledge.

39  Information on this instrument can be found at https://www.sigmaassessmentsystems.com/wp-content/uploads/2015/02/LCIA-360-Sample-Report.pdf

40  Amagoh, F. (2009). Leadership development and leadership effectiveness. *Management Decision. 47*(6), 989-999. (p. 990).

41  Researchers have determined that leaders can be developed through a conceptually strong program of leader development. They also suggest that developing leaders benefit significantly from challenging experiences early in their careers, strong mentors who provide guidance as well as feedback on leader performance, experience with both effective and ineffective leaders and the learning that can be garnered from  reflecting on the effective and ineffective practices of both types of leaders, and learning on how to effectively reflect on situations and make future plans accordingly. Readers are encouraged to review the informative work of LeBoeuf, J.N., et al (2004). Leaders are made, not born. The critical role of a developmental framework to facilitate an organizational culture of development. *Consulting Psychology Journal: Practice and Research. 56,* 1, 10-19.

42  Readers are encouraged to consult the formative work of David Day on leader and leadership development. In particular, readers should review Day D.V. (2000). Leadership development: A review in context, *The*

*Leadership Quarterly, 11*, 581-613 and Day, Fleenor, Atwater, Strum, & McKee (2014). Advances in leader and leadership development: A review of 25 years of research and theory. *The Leadership Quarterly, 25*, 63-82 for an historical overview of key research in this critical area.

43    See Hernez-Broome, G., & Hughes, R. J., (2004). Leadership development: Past, present, and future. *Human Resource Planning, 27*(1), 24-32

44    Kotter, J. P. (2008). *Force for change: How leadership differs from management.* Simon and Schuster.

45    Readers are encouraged to review the exciting leader development research of Liu, Z., Venkatesh, S., Murphy, S. E., & Riggio, R. E. (2021). Leader development across the lifespan: A dynamic experiences-grounded approach. *The Leadership Quarterly, 32*(5), 101382 and Boak, G., & Crabbe, S. (2019). Experiences that develop leadership capabilities. *Leadership & Organization Development Journal, 40*(1), 97-106 DOI 10.1108/LODJ-07-2018-0254

46    Day, D. V., Riggio, R. E., Tan, S. J., & Conger, J. A. (2021). Advancing the science of 21st-century leadership development: theory, research, and practice. *The Leadership Quarterly, 32*(5), p. 101557.

        Liu, Z., Venkatesh, S. Murphy, S. E., &, Riggio, R. E. (2021). Leader development across the lifespan: A dynamic experiences-grounded approach. *The Leadership Quarterly, 32*(5), p. 101382. doi.org/10.1016/j.leaqua.2020.101382.

47    Mertz, N. T. (2004). What's a mentor, anyway?. *Educational Administration Quarterly, 40*(4), 541-560.

48    Ibid

49    Readers are encouraged to review the seminal work of Speizer, J. J. (1981). Role models, mentors, and sponsors: The elusive concepts. *Signs: Journal of Women in Culture and Society, 6*(4), 692-712 and Ayyala, M. S., Skarupski, K., Bodurtha, J. N., González-Fernández, M., Ishii, L. E., Fivush, B., & Levine, R. B. (2019). Mentorship is not enough: exploring sponsorship and its role in career advancement in academic medicine. *Academic Medicine, 94*(1), 94-100.

50    Avolio, B. J., Reichard, R. J., Hannah, S. T., Walumbwa, F. O., & Chan, A. (2009). A meta-analytic review of leadership impact research: Experimental and quasi-experimental studies. *The leadership quarterly, 20*(5), 764-784.

51    Paice, E., Heard, S., & Moss, F. (2002). How important are role models in making good doctors?. *Bmj, 325*(7366), 707-710.

52    Brown, M. E., & Treviño, L. K. (2014). Do role models matter? An investigation of role modeling as an antecedent of perceived ethical leadership. *Journal of Business Ethics, 122*(4), 587-598.

53  See Gibson, D. E. (2004). Role models in career development: New directions for theory and research. *Journal of Vocational Behavior, 65*(1), 134-156 as well as Speizer, J. J. (1981). Role models, mentors, and sponsors: The elusive concepts. *Signs: Journal of Women in Culture and Society, 6*(4), 692-712.

54  Appelbaum, S. H., Ritchie, S., & Shapiro, B. T. (1994). Mentoring revisited: An organizational behaviour construct. *Journal of Management Development.* 13(4), 62-72.

55  Dziczkowski, J. (2013, July). Mentoring and leadership development. In *The Educational Forum* (Vol. 77(3) pp. 351-360).

56  Ibid, p. 351-252.

57  Fagenson-Eland, E. A., Marks, M. A., & Amendola, K. L. (1997). Perceptions of mentoring relationships. *Journal of vocational behavior, 51*(1), 29-42.

58  Levinson, W., Kaufman, K., Clark, B., & Tolle, S. W. (1991). Mentors and role models for women in academic medicine. *Western Journal of Medicine, 154*(4), 423-426.

59  Ayoobzadeh, M., & Boies, K. (2020). From mentors to leaders: leader development outcomes for mentors. *Journal of Managerial Psychology.* 35(6)., 497-511.

60  Cao, J., & Yang, Y. C. (2013). What are mentoring and sponsoring and how do they impact organizations?.

61  Friday, E., Friday, S. S., & Green, A. L. (2004). A reconceptualization of mentoring and sponsoring. *Management Decision.* 42(5). 628-644.

62  Brooks, D. (2019). *The second mountain: The quest for a moral life.* Random House, p. 104

63  Levinson (et al., 1991).

64  Appelbaum, S. H., Ritchie, S., & Shapiro, B. T. (1994). Mentoring revisited: An organizational behaviour construct. *Journal of Management Development.* 13(4), 62-72. (p. 70)

65  Helms, M. M., Arfken, D. E., & Bellar, S. (2016). The importance of mentoring and sponsorship in women's career development. *SAM advanced management journal, 81*(3), 4-16.

66  Singh, S., & Vanka, S. (2020). Mentoring is essential but not sufficient: sponsor women for leadership roles. *Development and Learning in Organizations: An International Journal.*34(6), 25-28.

67  Singh, S., & Vanka, S. (2020). Mentoring is essential but not sufficient: sponsor women for leadership roles. *Development and Learning in Organizations: An International Journal.*34(6), 25-28.

68  Ibid, p. 26.

69  Allen, K., Jacobson, S., & Lomotey, K. (1995). African American women in educational administration: The importance of mentors and sponsors. *Journal of Negro Education, 64*(4)409-422.

70  Bowness (2017, p. 190)

71  Ibid, p. 420

72  Cohen, A. R. (2004). Building a company of leaders. *Leader to Leader,* (34), 16-20.

73  Skipton Leonard, H., & Lang, F. (2010). Leadership development via action learning. *Advances in Developing Human Resources, 12*(2), 225-240.

74  Readers are encouraged to review the foundational work in this area and especially the work of Jay Conger and David Day. In particular, readers are encouraged to read Conger, J. A. (1992). *Learning to Lead: The Art of Transforming Managers into Leaders.* Jossey-Bass, and consult the formative work of David Day on leader and leadership development. In particular, readers should review Day D.V. (2000). Leadership development: A review in context, *The Leadership Quarterly, 11,* 581-613 and Day, Fleenor, Atwater, Strum, & McKee (2014). Advances in leader and leadership development: A review of 25 years of research and theory. *The Leadership Quarterly, 25,* 63-82 for an historical overview of key research in this critical area.

75  Lacerenza, C. N., Reyes, D. L., Marlow, S. L., Joseph, D. L., & Salas, E. (2017). Leadership training design, delivery, and implementation: A meta-analysis. *Journal of Applied Psychology, 102*(12), 1686, and Day, Fleenor, Atwater, Strum, & McKee (2014). Advances in leader and leadership development: A review of 25 years of research and theory. *The Leadership Quarterly, 25,* 63-82

76  Lacerenza, C. N., Reyes, D. L., Marlow, S. L., Joseph, D. L., & Salas, E. (2017). Leadership training design, delivery, and implementation: A meta-analysis. *Journal of Applied Psychology, 102*(12), 1686.

## Gear 2 - The Launch and Maturity Phase

77  Campbell, D. J., & Dardis, G. J. (2004). The "Be, Know, Do" model of leader development. *Human Resource Planning, 27*(2), 26-39.

78  Ibid

79  Fulmer, R. M., Stumpf, S. A., & Bleak, J. (2009). The strategic development of high potential leaders. *Strategy & Leadership.* 37(3), 17-22. (p. 19)

80  See Moldoveanu, M., & Narayandas, D. (2019). The future of leadership development. *Harvard Business Review, 97*(2), 40-48.

81 Contemporary leadership theorists are aligned on the need for a team approach to leadership and the basis on my recent book by Weese, W.J. (2018). *The 5C leader: Exceptional leadership practices for extraordinary times.* New York: Archway Publishing, a Division of Simon and Schuster, New York. NY. A team approach to leadership is also the central them of popular leadership books from contemporary authors like Lencioni, P. (2002). *The five dysfunctions of a team.* San Francisco, CA: Jossey-Bass; Lencioni, P. (2016). *The ideal team player: How to recognize and cultivate the three essential virtues.* Hoeboken, NJ: Jossey-Bass; Sinek, S. (2009). *Start with why: How great leaders inspire everyone to take action.* New York: Penguin Books, and; Sinek, S. (2014). *Leaders eat last: Why some teams pull together and others don't.* New York: Penguin Books.

82 Readers seeking to better understand the predictability of demographics and its impact on many sectors and encouraged to read Foot, D. K. (1996). *Boom, bust and echo: How to profit from the coming demographic shift.* MacFarland, Walter & Ross.

83 Lencioni, P. (2002). *The five dysfunctions of a team.* San Francisco, CA: Jossey-Bass; Lencioni, P. (2016). *The ideal team player: How to recognize and cultivate the three essential virtues.* Hoeboken, NJ: Jossey-Bass; Sinek, S. (2009). *Start with why: How great leaders inspire everyone to take action.* New York: Penguin Books, and; Sinek, S. (2014). *Leaders eat last: Why some teams pull together and others don't.* New York: Penguin Books.

84 Readers are encouraged to review Cohn, J., & Moran, J. (2011). *Why are we so bad at picking good leaders? A better way to evaluate leadership potential.* Jossey-Bass. I have long believed that this book would be even more impactful if it was titled: *Why are we so good at picking bad leaders?*

85 See Seijts, G. (2014). *Good leaders learn: Lessons from lifetimes of leadership.* New York: Routledge.

86 See Brown, J. (2019). *How to be an inclusive leader: Creating trust, cooperation, and community across differences.* Berrett-Koehler Publishers, and Fuller, P., Murphy, M., & Chow, A. (2020). *The leader's guide to unconscious bias: How to reframe bias, cultivate correction, and create high-performing teams.* Simon & Schuster.

87 Ibid

88 Lencioni, P. (2002). *The five dysfunctions of a team.* San Francisco, CA: Jossey-Bass; Lencioni, P. (2016). *The ideal team player: How to recognize and cultivate the three essential virtues.* Hoeboken, NJ: Jossey-Bass.

89 Watkins, M. (2013). *The First 90 Days – Proven Strategies for Getting Up to Speed Faster and Smarter,* Boston: Harvard Business.

90  See Goldsmith, M. (2007). *What got you here won't get you the*re. New York, NY: Hyperion Books Inc.

91  (Lencioni, 2002, p. vii) in Lencioni, P. (2002). *The five dysfunctions of a team.* San Francisco, CA: Jossey-Bass p. vii)

92  Lencioni, P. (2016). *The ideal team player: How to recognize and cultivate the three essential virtues.* Hoeboken, NJ: Jossey-Bass.

93  See George, B. (2009). *7 lessons for leading in a* crisis. San Francisco, CA: Jossey-Bass.

94  Lencioni (2002; 2016)

95  See Kahneman, D. (2011). *Thinking fast and slow.* Random House Canada.

96  Susan Cain provides a clear and compelling case that introverts are often (and erroneously) overlooked. Readers are encouraged to review her exceptional text. Cain, S. (2012). *Quiet: The power of introverts in a world that can't stop talking.* Random House.

97  Lencioni (2002)

98  Lencioni (2002, p. viii)

99  Lencioni (2002; 2016)

100 Readers are encouraged to read the work of Davey, L. (2019). *The good fight. Use productive conflict to get your team and organization back on track.* Raincoast Books; Leslie, I. (2021). *Conflicted: How productive disagreements lead to better outcomes.* Harper Business, and Sinek, S. (2014). *Leaders eat last: Why some teams pull together and others don't.* Penguin Books. These three sources, and others provide exceptional commentary on how conflict can be productivity channelled by leaders to help ensure better decisions and heightened unit effectiveness.

101 Readers are encouraged to read an informative book Tichy, N. M., and Bennis, W. G. (2007). *Judgement: How winning leaders make great calls.* Portfolio Group. In this book, Tichy and Bennis effectively and convincingly underscore the fact that leaders must make great decisions, and in many ways, are judged on the basis of the outcome of those decisions.

102 Obama, B. (2020). *A Promised Land.* Crown

103 Tichy, N. M., and Bennis, W. G. (2007). *Judgement: How winning leaders make great calls.* Portfolio Group

104 See Kahneman, D. (2011). *Thinking fast and slow.* Random House Canada.

105 Readers are encouraged to review the insightful works of Simon Sinek, and especially his 2009 book: Sinek, S. (2009). *Start with why: How great leaders inspire everyone to take action.* Portfolio.

106 Collins, J., & Hansen, M. T. (2011). *Great by choice: Uncertainty, chaos, and luck – why some thrive despite them all.* Harper and Collins.

107 Readers and encouraged to read these two books and employ the strategies that the authors outline to help get off to a great start. Jennings, J. (2009). *Hit the ground running: A manual for new leaders*. Penguin Books. Watkins, M. (2013). *The First 90 Days – Proven Strategies for Getting Up to Speed Faster and Smarter,* Boston: Harvard Business.

108 Review the work of the following authors for additional support for this claim. Brown, J. (2019). *How to be an inclusive leader: Creating trust, cooperation, and community across differences*. Berrett-Koehler Publishers; Goleman, D. (2013). *What makes a leader? Why emotional intelligence matters*. More than Sound;

109 Goleman, D. (2019). *The emotionally intelligent leader*. Harvard Business Review Press; Goleman, D., Boyatzis, R., & McKee, A. (2013). *Primal leadership: Realizing the power of emotional intelligence*. Harvard Business School Press; Nadler, R. S. (2010). *Leading with emotional intelligence: Hands-on strategies for building confident and collaborative star performers*. McGraw-Hill, and, Seijts, G. (2014). *Good leaders learn: Lessons from a lifetime of leadership*. Routledge 109 Boyatzis and McKee (2005, p. 4) in Boyatzis, R., & McKee, A. (2005). *Resonant leadership*. Harvard Business School Press.

110 Goleman, D. (2013). *What makes a leader? Why emotional intelligence matters*. More than Sound.

111 Boyatzis, R. (2009, October). *Emotional intelligence*. Paper presented at the 2009 Global Institute for Leadership Development. San Diego.

112 See Brooks, D. (2019). *The second mountain: The quest for a moral life*. Random House.

113 Ibid

114 See Keller, G., & Papasan, J. (2012). *The one thing: The surprising simple truth behind extraordinary results*. Bard Press.

115 Bennis, W., & Ward Biederman, P. (2010). *Still surprised: A memoir of a life in leadership*. San Francisco: Jossey-Bass; Parks. S. D. (2005). *Leadership can be taught*. Harvard Business School Press, and; Seijts, G. (2014). *Good leaders learn: Lessons from a lifetime of leadership*. Routledge.

116 One of the most impactful leadership books that I have read was authored by Stew Friedman from the Wharton School of Business at Penn. Friedman convincingly highlights the need to integrate leadership roles (personal, family, career, community) into an overlapping concept appropriately titled "Total Leadership". Readers are encouraged to read his insightful book Friedman, S. (2008). *Total leadership: Be a better leader, have a richer life*. Harvard Business School Press.

117 Friedman (2008, p. 187)

118 George, B. (2009). *7 lessons for leading in a crisis*. Jossey-Bass.

## Gear 3 - The Rebirth/Renewal or Time to Exit Phase

119 [1] See Earley, P., & Weindling, D. (2007). Do school leaders have a shelf life? Career stages and headteacher performance. *Educational Management Administration & Leadership, 35*(1), 73-88.

120 Atton, T., & Fidler, B. (2003). *The headship game: The challenges of contemporary school leadership*. Routledge.

121 Henderson, A. D., Miller, D., & Hambrick, D. C. (2006). How quickly do CEOs become obsolete? Industry dynamism, CEO tenure, and company performance. *Strategic Management Journal, 27*(5), 447-460.

122 See https://www.pwc.com/gx/en/news-room/press-releases/2019/ceo-turnover-record-high.html#:~:text=The%20study%2C%20which%20analyzed%20CEO,over%20the%20time%20period%20analyzed.

123 Few studies have focused on this portion of the leadership lifecycle. Readers interested in the topic will enjoy reading Henderson, A. D., Miller, D., & Hambrick, D. C. (2006). How quickly do CEOs become obsolete? Industry dynamism, CEO tenure, and company performance. *Strategic Management Journal, 27*(5), 447–460. https://doi.org/10.1002/smj.524

Redman, R.W. (2006). Leadership succession planning: An evidence-based approach for managing the future. *The Journal of Nursing Administration, 36(6),* 292-297.

Robinson, C. (2013, August 16). *Leadership shelf life*. Retrieved May 11, 2019, from https://www.vantageleadership.com/our-blog/carl-robinson-on-leadership-shelf-life/Zucco, A. (2015, July 15). *Leadership has a shelf life: How to make sure your leadership approach hasn't gone stale*. https://cvdl.ben.edu/blog/leadership-shelf-life-leadership-approach-hasnt-stale/

124 Readers are encouraged to read the insighted book by Stanley Bing who draws parallels of the leadership lifecycle to bread going stale. Bing, S. (2003). *The big bing: Black holes of time management, gaseous executive bodies, exploding careers, and other theories on the origins of the business universe*. Harper and Collins.

125 Sills, J. (2004). *The comfort trap, or what if I am riding a dead horse?* Viking Adult.

126 Bing (2003)

127 Goleman, D. (2019). *The emotionally intelligent leader*. Harvard Business Review Press and Goleman, D., Boyatzis, R., & McKee, A. (2013). *Primal*

*leadership: Realizing the power of emotional intelligence.* Harvard Business School Press.

128 See Day, D. V., Riggio, R. E., Tan, S. J., & Conger, J. A. (2021). Advancing the science of 21ˢᵗ-century leadership development: Theory, research, and practice. *The Leadership Quarterly, 32*(5),101557, https://doi.org/10.1016/j. leaqua.2021.101557. See Liu, Z., Venkatesh, S., Murphy, S. E., & Riggio, R. E. (2021). Leader development across the lifespan: A dynamic experiences-grounded approach. The Leadership Quarterly, 32(5), 101382. https://doi.org/10.1016/j.leaqua.2020.101382.

129 Goleman, D. (2019). *The emotionally intelligent leader.* Harvard Business Review Press and Goleman, D., Boyatzis, R., & McKee, A. (2013). *Primal leadership: Realizing the power of emotional intelligence.* Harvard Business School Press.

130 Percy, L., & Rossiter, J. R. (1992). A model of brand awareness and brand attitude advertising strategies. *Psychology & Marketing, 9*(4), 263-274.

131 Readers are encouraged to review the insightful article by Jacobus, W. P. (2011). What lurks beneath leadership ineffectiveness? A theoretical over-view. *African Journal of Business Management, 5*(26), 10629-10633

132 Pienaar, C. (2009). The role of self-deception in leadership ineffective-ness—a theoretical overview. *South African Journal of Psychology, 39*(1), 133-141.

133 I consider the Tichy, N. M., & Cohen, E. (2002). *The leadership engine: How winning companies build leaders at every level.* New York: Harper Collins to be one of the most impactful leadership books of my generation. I write about the importance of passion in my The 5C Leader book. Tichy and Cohen write extensively about the need for leaders to have "edge". When it goes, so does a leaders impact and to me it is a blue-ribbon indicator of a time for a leader to step aside from the leadership role and turn it over to others with the requisite level of passion and edge.

134 See Kahneman, D. (2011). *Thinking fast and slow.* Random House Canada and the work of Daniel Goleman and colleagues - Goleman, D. (2019). *The emotionally intelligent leader.* Harvard Business Review Press; Goleman, D., Boyatzis, R., & McKee, A. (2013). *Primal leadership: Realizing the power of emotional intelligence.* Harvard Business School Press; and Nadler, R. S. (2010). *Leading with emotional intelligence: Hands-on strategies for building confident and collaborative star performers.* McGraw-Hill. These clairvoy-ant writers cover the concept of self-awareness and its centrality to emo-tional intelligence and leadership effectiveness. Leaders can also use their research to sharpen their acuity and make more accurate assessments of

their passion for leadership, their openness to new ideas and learning, and ultimately, their decision to leave the leadership role at the right time.

135 See Sills, J. (2004). *The Comfort Trap, Or, What If You're Riding a Dead Horse?*. Viking Adult.

136 See Collins, J., & Hansen, M. T. (2011). *Great by choice: Uncertainty, chaos, and luck – why some thrive despite them all*. Harper and Collins.

137 Weese covers this process thoroughly in his Weese, W.J. (2018). *The 5C leader: Exceptional leadership practices for extraordinary times*. New York: Archway Publishing, a Division of Simon and Schuster book. Readers are encouraged to review the contents of that book for a better understanding of how to effectively engage colleagues and inspire ground-up visions.

138 Readers will not find many sources dedicated to the end stage of the leadership lifecycle. Two exceptions would be the insightful work of Kerfoot, K. (2004). The shelf life of leaders. *Dermatology Nursing, 16*(4), 379-381 as well as the research of Hargreaves, A., & Fink, D. (2012). *Sustainable leadership* (Vol. 6). John Wiley & Sons.

139 Readers are encouraged to review the insightful leader sustainability suggestions offered by Ulrich, D., & Smallwood, N. (2013). Leadership sustainability. *Leader to Leader, 2013*(70), 32–38. https://doi.org/10.1002/ltl.20098

140 Ulrich, D., & Smallwood, N. (2013). Leadership sustainability. *Leader to Leader, 2013*(70), 32–38. https://doi.org/10.1002/ltl.20098

141 Lipiner, B. (2020, December 10) Do leaders have a shelf life? Not if they follow this advice. Accessed at: https://entrepreneurship.babson.edu/do-leaders-have-shelf-life/

142 Boyatzis, R., Boyatzis, R. E., & McKee, A. (2005). *Resonant leadership: Renewing yourself and connecting with others through mindfulness, hope, and compassion*. Harvard Business Press.

143 Ulrich, D., & Smallwood, N. (2013). Leadership sustainability. *Leader to Leader, 2013*(70), 32–38. https://doi.org/10.1002/ltl.20098

144 Goldsmith, M. (2009). *Succession: Are you Ready?* Harvard Business Press and Goldsmith (2009); Ulrich, D., & Smallwood, N. (2013). Leadership sustainability. *Leader to Leader, 2013*(70), 32–38. https://doi.org/10.1002/ltl.20098

145 Goleman, D. (2019). *The emotionally intelligent leader*. Harvard Business Review Press; Goleman, D., Boyatzis, R., & McKee, A. (2013). *Primal leadership: Realizing the power of emotional intelligence*. Harvard Business School Press; and Nadler, R. S. (2010). *Leading with emotional intelligence: Hands-on strategies for building confident and collaborative star performers*. McGraw-Hill.

146 Weese covers this topic in C4 – Contagious Enthusiasm in his book. See Weese, W.J. (2018). *The 5C leader: Exceptional leadership practices for extraordinary times.* New York: Archway Publishing, a Division of Simon and Schuster book..

147 Hargreaves, A., & Fink, D. (2012). *Sustainable leadership* (Vol. 6). John Wiley & Sons.

148 Ulrich, D., & Smallwood, N. (2013, p. 37)

149 See Rosenthal, J., Routch, K., Monahan, K., & Doherty, M. (2018). The holy grail of effective leadership succession planning. Deloitte Insights, 1-11.

150 Readers are encouraged to review the insightful writing of Marshall Goldsmith. His book, Goldsmith, M. (2009). *Succession: Are you Ready?* Harvard Business Press is especially recommended for leaders seeking to better understand when and how to leave a leadership role.

151 See Brooks, D. (2019). *The second mountain: The quest for a moral life.* Random House.

152 Readers are encouraged to review the work of Zhengguang Liu, Z., Venkatesh, S., Murphy, S. E., and Riggio, R.E. (2021). Leader development across the lifespan: A dynamic experiences-grounded approach, *The Leadership Quarterly, 32(5),* https://doi.org/10.1016/j.leaqua.2020.101382.

153 Kim, T. H. (2012). Succession planning in hospitals and the association with organizational performance. *Nursing Economics, 30*(1), 14-20 (p. 15)

154 Shirey, M. R. (2008). Building the leadership development pipeline: A 5-step succession planning model. *Clinical Nurse Specialist, 22*(5), 214-217. (p. 214).

155 Ndunguru, C. A. (2012). Executive onboarding: How to hit the ground running. *Public manager, 41*(3), 6-9. (p. 6)

156 Ross, W. E., Huang, K. H., & Jones, G. H. (2014). Executive onboarding: ensuring the success of the newly hired department chair. *Academic Medicine, 89*(5), 728-733.

157 Ibid

158 Goldsmith (2009)

159 Dai, G., & De Meuse, K. P. (2007). A review of onboarding literature. *Lominger Limited, Inc., a subsidiary of Korn/Ferry International,* 1-9.

160 See Kotter, J. P. (2012). *Leading change.* Boston, MA: Harvard Business Press.

161 Hall-Ellis, S. D. (2014). Onboarding to improve library retention and productivity. *The Bottom Line.* (p. 138).

162 Leaders struggling with the decision to step away because they are worried about what they might do next would be comforted by the insightful suggestions offered by David Brooks in his recent book Brooks, D. (2019). *The*

*second mountain: The quest for a moral life.* Random House. Many leaders hold on to roles well beyond their best before date because they are unsure of what to do next. Brooks' comforting words will help these individuals realize that they have so much more to offer other groups and organizations, and make other contributions.

163 Goldsmith (2009)
164 Ibid
165 Ibid
166 Goldsmith (2009, p. 26).

## Conclusion

167 Boles, R. N. (1978). *The boxes of life and how to get out of them.* Ten Speed Press.

# SUGGESTED READING

Bass, B. M. (1990). *Bass and Stogdill's handbook of leadership: Theory, research and managerial applications.* Free Press.

Beard, S., & Weese, W. J. (2020). A 50-year retrospective of leadership development through varsity sport from the former athletes' perspective. *Journal for the Study of Sports and Athletics in Education,* 1-25. doi.org/10.1080/19357397.2020.1774238

Beatty, J. (1998). *The world according to Peter Drucker.* The Free Press.

Bennis, W. (2009). *The essential Bennis.* Wiley.

Bennis, W., Goleman, D., & Ward Biederman, P. (2008). Creating a culture of candor. In W. Bennis, D. Goleman, J. Toole (Eds). *How leaders create a culture of candor.* (pp.1-43). Jossey-Bass.

Bennis, W. G., & Thomas, R. J. (2007). *Leading for a lifetime.* Boston, MA: Harvard Business School Publishing.

Bennis, W., & Ward Biederman, P. (2010). *Still surprized: A memoir of a life in leadership.* Jossey-Bass.

Boles, R. N. (1978). *The boxes of life and how to get out of them.* Ten Speed Press.

Boyatzis, R., & McKee, A. (2005). *Resonant leadership.* Harvard Business School Press.

Brooks, D. (2015). *The Road to Character.* Random House.

Brooks, D. (2019). *The second mountain: The quest for a moral life.* Random House.

Brungardt, C. (1996). The making of leaders: A review of the research in leadership development and education. *Journal of Leadership Studies, 3*(3), 81-95.

Bryman, A. (1992). *Charisma and leadership in organizations.* Sage.

Cain, S. (2012). *Quiet: The power of introverts in a world that can't stop talking.* Random House.

Cohn, J., & Moran, J. (2011). Why are we so bad at picking good leaders? A better way to evaluate leadership potential. Jossey-Bass.

Collins, J., & Hansen, M. T. (2011). *Great by choice: Uncertainty, chaos, and luck: Why some thrive despite them all.* Harper and Collins.

Conger, J. A. (1989). *The charismatic leader: Behind the mystique of exceptional leadership.* Jossey-Bass.

Covey, S. (1989). *The 7 habits of highly effective people.* Simon & Schuster.

Covey, S. R. (1991). *Principled-centered leadership*. Summit.

Crossan, M., Seijts, G., & Gandz, J. (2015). *Developing leadership character*. Routledge.

Cuddy, A. (2015). *Presence: Bring your boldest self to your biggest challenge*. Little, Brown and Company.

Day, D. V., & Dragoni, L. (2015). Leadership development: An outcome-oriented review based on time and levels of analyses. *Annual Review of Organizational Psychology and Organizational Behavior, 2*(1) 133-156.

Friedman, S. (2008). *Total leadership: Be a better leader, have a richer life*. Harvard Business School Press.

George, B. (2009). *7 lessons for leading in a crisis*. Jossey-Bass.

Goldsmith, M. (2007). *What got you here won't get you there*. Hyperion Books Inc.

Goldsmith, M. (2009). *Succession: Are you Ready?* Harvard Business Press.

Goleman, D. (2013). *What makes a leader? Why emotional intelligence matters*. More than Sound.

Goleman, D. (2019). *The emotionally intelligent leader*. Harvard Business Review Press.

Goleman, D., Boyatzis, R., & McKee, A. (2013). *Primal leadership: Realizing the power of emotional intelligence*. Harvard Business School Press.

Jennings, J. (2009). *Hit the ground running: A manual for new leaders.* Penguin Books.

Kahneman, D. (2011). *Thinking fast and slow.* Random House Canada.

Lencioni, P. (2002). *The five dysfunctions of a team.* Jossey-Bass.

Lencioni, P. (2016). *The ideal team player: How to recognize and cultivate the three Essential virtues.* Jossey-Bass.

Mintzberg, H. (1989). *Mintzberg on management: Inside our strange world of organizations.* The Free Press.

Nadler, R. S. (2010). *Leading with emotional intelligence: Hands-on strategies for Building confident and collaborative star performers.* McGraw-Hill.

Obama, B. (2020). *A Promised Land.* Crown.

Parks. S. D. (2005). *Leadership can be taught.* Harvard Business School Press.

Scott, D. (2021). *Contemporary leadership in sport organizations.* Human Kinetics.

Seijts, G. (2014). *Good leaders learn: Lessons from a lifetime of leadership.* Routledge.

Sinek, S. (2009). *Start with why: How great leaders inspire everyone to take action.* Penguin Books.

Sinek, S. (2014). *Leaders eat last: Why some teams pull together and others don't.* Penguin Books.

Tichy, N. M., and Bennis, W. G. (2007). *Judgement: How winning leaders make great calls.* Portfolio Group.

Tichy, N. M., & Cohen, E. (2002). *The leadership engine: How winning companies build leaders at every level.* Harper Collins.

Weese, W. J. (2018). *The 5C leader: Exceptional leadership practices for extraordinary times.* Archway Publishing, a Division of Simon and Schuster.

Welty Peachey, J., Damon, Z., Zhou, Y., & Burton, L. J. (2015). Forty years of leadership research in sport management; A review, synthesis, and conceptual framework. *Journal of Sport Management, 29,* 570-578.

Yukl, G. A. (1989). *Leadership in organizations.* Englewood Cliffs, NJ: Prentice-Hall.

Yukl, G. A. (1989). Managerial leadership: A review of theory and research. *Journal of Management, 15*(2), 251-289.

# INDEX

www.ingramcontent.com/pod-product-compliance
Lightning Source LLC
Chambersburg PA
CBHW021405210526
45463CB00001B/224